Healthy Home Cooking

❧ ❧ ❧

Quick & Healthy Low-Fat Cooking
from the Food Editors of
PREVENTION Magazine

Rodale Press, Inc.
Emmaus, Pennsylvania

QUICK AND HEALTHY LOW-FAT COOKING

Managing Editor: JEAN ROGERS
Executive Editor: DEBORA A. TKAC
Senior Book Designer: ELIZABETH OTWELL
Art Director: JANE COLBY KNUTILA
Associate Art Director: FAITH HAGUE

Healthy Home Cooking was produced by Rebus, Inc.
Recipe Development: MIRIAM RUBIN
Writer and Recipe Editor: BONNIE J. SLOTNICK
Art Director and Designer: JUDITH HENRY
Production Editor: SUE PAIGE

Photographer: ELLEN SILVERMAN
Nutritional analyses: HILL NUTRITION ASSOCIATES

Library of Congress Cataloging-in-Publication Data

Healthy home cooking: family favorites old and new for today's health-
  conscious cooks.
    p.   cm. — (quick & healthy low-fat cooking)
    Includes index.
    ISBN 0–87596–276–9   hardcover
    ISBN 0–87596–244–0   paperback
    1. Cookery.   2. Low-fat diet—Recipes.   3. Low-cholesterol diet—
Recipes.   4. Quick and easy cookery.   I. Prevention
(Emmaus, Pa.)
II. Series.
TX714.H395   1995
641.5—dc20   94–44421

Distributed in the book trade by St. Martin's Press

2   4   6   8   10   9   7   5   3   1   hardcover
2   4   6   8   10   9   7   5   3   1   paperback

CONTENTS

❧ ❧ ❧

PREFACE

❧ ❧ ❧

For many people, the thought of having to forsake the comfort foods they grew up on—or the old standbys they really love to eat—is the major reason to resist changing their diets for the better. Fortunately, that sort of deprivation really *isn't* necessary. Often, all they need to do is make a few minor changes in the way the food is prepared.

The recipes in this book show you how to make these changes, capitalizing on the secrets used by health-conscious cooks to cut fat but keep flavor. The recipes fall into two categories: There are classic favorites (such as fried chicken and brownies), artfully updated with an eye toward preserving their familiar, delicious taste; and new takes on homestyle dishes that can expand your culinary repertoire. Included are appealing versions of chowder, chili and chops, side dishes and salads, pie, pudding and more. Both types of recipes can help you embrace a healthy eating plan, because it's important that you—and your family—*like* what you eat. Denying yourself the pleasures of enjoyable food just never works. In fact, it could set you up for a backlash that scuttles all your best intentions.

There are dozens of reasons to follow a healthful diet. Many people, for instance, want to look good by losing extra pounds and hope to avoid such nutrition- and weight-related ailments as heart disease and adult-onset diabetes (over half of the top ten killer diseases in this country are related to what we eat). Still others just want to feel more energized—they're too busy to let less-than-optimum nutrition slow them down.

No matter what your reasons for eating smart, you can depend on the recipes in *Healthy Home Cooking* to satisfy your cravings for hearty old-fashioned food *and* pay you health dividends that'll last a lifetime.

Jean Rogers

JEAN ROGERS
Food Editor
Prevention Magazine Health Books

INTRODUCTION

❧ ❧ ❧

When the family comes home from a day at work, school or weekend play, it isn't carrot sticks or a bowl of broth they'll be clamoring for. They'll want real food, hearty food—preferably familiar dishes that they've come to love over the years. Can you fulfill this hunger for homestyle cooking without serving up too much fat, cholesterol and salt—and without spending hours in the kitchen cooking and cleaning up?

With *Healthy Home Cooking,* you can. This book shows you how to trim down those family favorites and also introduces some new homestyle meals that will fit perfectly—and deliciously—into the busy schedules of today's families.

Perhaps the most important concept in reducing the fat content of a classic dish lies in shifting the focus so that more calories come from carbohydrates, especially complex carbohydrates (starches), than from fat or protein. Take that universal favorite, macaroni and cheese, as an example: A standard recipe to serve four people calls for equal amounts of pasta and cheese, plus eggs, whole milk and a topping of buttered bread crumbs and grated cheese. This casserole comes laden with more than 30 grams of fat per serving. To lighten the recipe, use more pasta and less cheese, and add some vegetables to the dish. The recipe for Baked Shells with White Cheddar (page 101), created along these lines, boasts a creamy sauce made from skim milk and cottage cheese; mustard and hot-pepper sauce point up the inimitable flavor of sharp Cheddar, and spinach is stirred into the sauce before the pasta is baked. The result is an undeniably delicious dish with just under 14 grams of fat per serving.

The same "tipping the balance" theory can be applied to stews (use less beef and more potatoes and carrots), steak dinners (pair sliced sirloin with lots of colorful sautéed bell peppers) and even desserts (top an abundant serving of fruit with frozen yogurt rather than garnishing a bowl of premium ice cream with a single cherry). And these aren't just theoretical cases: You'll find the recipes for these very "makeovers" on the pages of this book.

The substitution of low-fat ingredients is another route to healthier meals. Leaner cuts of meat, low-fat dairy products and egg whites instead of whole eggs can be introduced in standard recipes, although it may take a bit of experimentation. When lightening your own recipes, start by removing (or replacing) high-fat ingredients a little at a time until you find out how much alteration the dish can tolerate.

Of course, there will be times when you want to go all-out—to serve a lavishly frosted layer cake for a birthday party or share your great-grandmother's old-world lasagna at a family reunion. If your everyday meals are as wholesome as those you'll find within these pages, there's no reason not to enjoy the occasional splurge.

The next few pages of this book present healthy transformations of some of America's best-beloved foods, including brownies and pizza. These recipes demonstrate some principles of healthier cooking that you can apply to your own favorite recipes: Bake rather than fry; use turkey or chicken instead of red meat; substitute yogurt for mayonnaise and sour cream; replace some of the fat in cookies and cakes with applesauce or yogurt.

On pages 14 and 15, you'll find a glossary of equipment that can help you minimize the fat in your diet while maximizing the flavor in your meals. You may already have some of these tools in your kitchen; if not, they're a small but worthwhile investment in your family's health and eating pleasure.

OVEN-FRIED CHICKEN

❧ ❧ ❧

Instead of frying chicken in several cups of fat, you can bake these slightly spicy, crisp-crusted chicken parts using only 2 teaspoons of oil.

  1 **cup unseasoned dry bread crumbs**

  ½ **cup plain nonfat yogurt**

  2 **garlic cloves, crushed**

  2 **teaspoons cider vinegar**

  ½ **teaspoon hot-pepper sauce**

  1½ **pounds skinned chicken legs, drumsticks and thighs cut apart**

  2 **teaspoons canola oil**

1 Preheat the oven to 450°. Spray a jelly-roll pan with no-stick spray. Spread the breadcrumbs in a shallow plate.

2 In a large bowl, stir together the yogurt, garlic, vinegar and hot-pepper sauce. Add the chicken pieces and toss to coat well. One piece at time, transfer the chicken pieces to the plate of breadcrumbs and dredge them in the crumbs to coat evenly. Arrange the chicken in a single layer on the prepared pan.

3 Drizzle the oil over the chicken and bake for 30 to 35 minutes, or until the chicken is browned and no longer pink near the bone.

Per serving 286 calories, 8.4 g. fat, 1.7 g. saturated fat, 93 mg. cholesterol, 370 mg. sodium **Serves 4**

CHILI-GLAZED MINI MEAT LOAVES

❧ ❧ ❧

Almost any ground-beef recipe can be made more healthful by replacing all or part of the beef with ground chicken breast or turkey breast.

½ small onion, cut into chunks

2 tablespoons parsley sprigs

1 garlic clove, peeled

8 ounces lean, trimmed beef top round, cut into chunks

8 ounces skinless chicken breast, cut into chunks

¼ cup unseasoned dry bread crumbs

¼ cup chili sauce

1 large egg white

1 tablespoon skim milk

½ teaspoon dried thyme, crumbled

¼ teaspoon freshly ground black pepper

⅛ teaspoon salt

1 Preheat the oven to 400°. Spray a 9 x 13-inch baking pan with no-stick spray.

2 Place the onions, parsley and garlic in a food processor, and process until finely chopped. Add the beef and chicken chunks, and process until ground. Add the bread crumbs, 2 tablespoons of the chili sauce, the egg white, milk, thyme, pepper and salt, and pulse until the mixture is well blended.

3 Divide the meat mixture into 4 equal portions and shape each portion into a small oval loaf. Place the meat loaves in the prepared pan, leaving space between them. Bake the meat loaves for 20 minutes.

4 Brush the tops of the meat loaves with the remaining 2 tablespoons chili sauce and bake them for 5 minutes longer, or until browned; a meat thermometer inserted in the center of one of the loaves should register 175°.

Per serving 197 calories, 3.3 g. fat, 0.9 g. saturated fat, 65 mg. cholesterol, 439 mg. sodium **Serves 4**

Tuna Salad

❧ ❧ ❧

You don't have to "hold the mayo"—just use a combination of reduced-calorie mayonnaise and nonfat yogurt. Add lots of diced vegetables and chick-peas to yield truly bountiful portions.

    2 cans (6⅛ ounces each) water-packed tuna

    1 can (10½ ounces) chick-peas

    1 large red bell pepper, diced

    ½ cup peeled, diced cucumber

    1 medium tomato, diced

    ¼ cup sliced scallions

    ⅓ cup plain nonfat yogurt

    3 tablespoons snipped fresh dill

    2 tablespoons reduced-calorie mayonnaise

    2 tablespoons fresh lemon juice

    ½ teaspoon freshly ground black pepper

    ½ teaspoon dry mustard

1 Drain the tuna, break it into chunks and place it in a strainer; rinse it under cold running water and drain again. Transfer the tuna to a serving bowl.

2 To the tuna, add the chick-peas, bell peppers, cucumbers, tomatoes and scallions, and toss gently. Add the yogurt, dill, mayonnaise, lemon juice, ground pepper and mustard, and stir until well mixed.

Per serving 243 calories, 3.5 g. fat, 0.7 g. saturated fat, 35 mg. cholesterol, 559 mg. sodium **Serves 4**

Spinach Pizza

❧ ❧ ❧

Easy on the cheese, generous with the vegetables— that's the way to make a guilt-free pizza. This one has a chewy herbed crust, a garlicky spinach topping and the rich flavor of sun-dried tomatoes.

 1½ teaspoons active dry yeast

    ½ teaspoon granulated sugar

    ¾ cup lukewarm water (105° to 115°)

 1¾ cups all-purpose flour

    2 tablespoons grated Parmesan cheese

    ½ teaspoon dried oregano, crumbled

    ¼ teaspoon fennel seeds

    ½ teaspoon freshly ground black pepper

    ¼ teaspoon salt

    2 ounces sun-dried tomatoes (not oil-packed)

    1 cup boiling water

    3 garlic cloves, thinly sliced

    1 teaspoon extra-virgin olive oil

    8 cups trimmed, loosely packed fresh spinach

    1 can (8 ounces) no-salt-added tomato sauce

    3 ounces shredded part-skim mozzarella cheese

    ⅛ teaspoon crushed red pepper flakes

1 In a small bowl, sprinkle the yeast and sugar over ¼ cup of the lukewarm water; stir until dissolved. Cover with plastic wrap and let stand for 5 to 10 minutes (the mixture should foam up).

2 Meanwhile, in a large bowl, mix the flour, 1 tablespoon of the Parmesan, the oregano, fennel seeds, ¼ teaspoon of the pepper and ⅛ teaspoon of the salt. Add the yeast mixture and the remaining ½ cup lukewarm water, and stir until a soft dough forms.

3 Gather the dough into a ball and knead on a lightly floured surface for 5 minutes, or until smooth and elastic. Spray a medium bowl with no-stick spray; place the dough in the bowl and turn to coat the dough with the spray. Cover the bowl with plastic wrap and let the dough rise in a warm place for 45 minutes, or until it is doubled in bulk.

4 Meanwhile, halve the sun-dried tomatoes. Place them in a small heatproof bowl and pour the boiling water over them. Let the tomatoes stand for 10 minutes, or until softened; drain and pat dry.

5 In a large no-stick skillet, mix the garlic cloves and oil. Place the skillet over high heat and sauté, stirring constantly, for 2 to 3 minutes, or until the garlic is lightly browned; transfer to a small plate.

6 Add half of the spinach to the skillet and stir-fry over high heat for 1 minute. Add the remaining spinach and stir-fry for 1 minute, or until wilted. Remove the skillet from the heat; stir in the remaining ¼ teaspoon pepper and remaining ⅛ teaspoon salt.

7 Preheat the oven to 500°. Spray a large baking sheet or a 12-inch pizza pan with no-stick spray. On a floured surface, using a floured rolling pin, roll the dough out to a 12-inch circle. Transfer the dough to the prepared sheet or pan. (If using a baking sheet, roll and pinch the edge of the dough into a raised border; if using a pizza pan, press the dough up the sides.) Spread the tomato sauce over the dough and bake for 8 to 10 minutes, or until the crust is lightly browned and the sauce is bubbly.

8 Remove the pizza from the oven and top with the spinach mixture. Sprinkle with the sautéed garlic and place the sun-dried tomatoes on top. Scatter the mozzarella over the pizza, then sprinkle with the remaining 1 tablespoon Parmesan and the red pepper. Bake for another 10 minutes, or until the cheese is bubbly and the crust is golden. Cut the pizza into wedges to serve.

Per serving 382 calories, 7.4 g. fat, 3.2 g. saturated fat, 15 mg. cholesterol, 427 mg. sodium **Serves 4**

HERBED OVEN FRIES

❧ ❧ ❧

The next time you're tempted by fast-food french fries, consider baking a batch of these herbed potatoes instead: A medium portion of fast-food fries may be laden with as much as 20 grams of fat.

   1 **pound russet potatoes**

   1 **tablespoon chopped fresh Italian parsley**

1½ **teaspoons olive oil**

   ½ **teaspoon dried thyme, crumbled**

   ¼ **teaspoon freshly ground black pepper**

   ⅛ **teaspoon salt**

1 Preheat the oven to 450°. Spray a heavy baking sheet or jelly-roll pan with no-stick spray.

2 Scrub the potatoes and cut them into ½-inch-thick matchsticks. Pile the potato sticks in the center of the prepared baking sheet and sprinkle with the parsley, oil, thyme, pepper and salt. Toss to coat well, then spread the potatoes in an even layer.

3 Bake the potatoes, turning them several times, for 20 to 25 minutes, or until crisp and browned.

Per serving 110 calories, 2.2 g. fat, 0.2 g. saturated fat, 0 mg. cholesterol, 78 mg. sodium **Serves 4**

1/4 cup plain nonfat yogurt

1/4 cup frozen apple juice concentrate

1 large egg plus 2 large egg whites

2 tablespoons vegetable oil

2 teaspoons vanilla extract

1 square (1 ounce) semisweet chocolate, melted

1/8 teaspoon salt

1 Preheat the oven to 350°. Spray an 8 x 8-inch baking pan with no-stick spray.

2 In a large bowl, combine the flour, cocoa, baking powder and baking soda, and stir until well mixed; set aside.

3 In a medium bowl, whisk together the applesauce, sugar, yogurt, apple juice concentrate, whole egg, oil and vanilla, then whisk in the melted chocolate; set aside.

4 In another large bowl, using an electric mixer on high speed, beat the egg whites and salt just until stiff, glossy (but not dry) peaks form.

5 Stir the chocolate mixture into the flour mixture, then, using a rubber spatula, fold in the beaten egg whites. Scrape the mixture into the prepared pan and bake for 25 minutes, or until a toothpick inserted in the center comes out clean.

6 Cool the brownies in the pan on a wire rack, then cut into 9 squares.

Per serving 183 calories, 5.2 g. fat, 1.4 g. saturated fat, 24 mg. cholesterol, 133 mg. sodium **Serves 9**

BROWNIES

S erious chocolate lovers—especially those who half-jokingly refer to themselves as "chocolate addicts"—find their favorite high-fat treat all but impossible to forgo. These cakelike brownies will fill the "chocolate gap" nicely, with a minimum of fat.

1 cup all-purpose flour

1/3 cup unsweetened cocoa powder

3/4 teaspoon baking powder

1/4 teaspoon baking soda

2/3 cup unsweetened applesauce

1/2 cup granulated sugar

THE SMART COOK'S TOOLS

❧ ❧ ❧

Dependable recipes and high-quality ingredients are just two components of healthy home cooking. A third factor is the right kitchen tools, which can spell the difference between success and failure, efficiency and waste. Some of the equipment described here makes the preparation of healthful foods, such as fruits and vegetables, less of a chore, while some of the implements actually enable you to reduce the fat content of the dishes you prepare.

STEAMER Steaming is hard to beat as a healthful cooking method, especially for vegetables. Because the food does not directly contact the water, most nutrients are conserved. And because food is not likely to stick, there's no need for added fat. Steaming works very well for fish fillets and chicken cutlets. The familiar (and inexpensive) collapsible vegetable steamer, set into a pot with a tight-fitting lid, is fine for small quantities of food; steamers with multiple stacking inserts—either the Chinese bamboo type or stainless steel ver-

sions—let you cook an entire meal at once. Specialized electric rice steamers turn out perfect rice (and vegetables, too). You can improvise your own steamer by crossing a pair of wooden chopsticks in the bottom of a deep pan or wok and setting a plate on top of them; a wire cake-cooling rack can be used in the same way.

YOGURT FUNNEL If you've been trying to reduce the fat in your diet, you're probably eating less whipped cream, cream cheese, sour cream and mayonnaise. It's possible, however, to make sauces, dips, spreads—even cheesecake—with yogurt: not yogurt spooned straight from the container, but yogurt that's been thickened by draining off the whey (the liquid part). This can be

done by placing the yogurt in an inexpensive mesh yogurt funnel, or you can improvise with a strainer lined with cheesecloth or a drip-style coffee filter fitted with a paper liner. Use low-fat or nonfat plain yogurt—or a "smooth" yogurt flavor

such as coffee, vanilla or lemon. After draining for an hour or two, plain yogurt is ready to stand in for sour cream; if you're making a spread, dip or creamy dessert, drain the yogurt overnight. Sweeten or season the yogurt as you like after draining. Refrigerate the yogurt-draining setup if you're letting it stand for more than a few minutes.

GRAVY STRAINER It's hard to do a thorough job of skimming the fat from a pot of gravy, soup or sauce. The easy way out is to use a gravy strainer or a fat-removing ladle. A gravy strainer looks like a plastic measuring cup with a spout that originates near the bottom of the cup: When you pour in liquid, any fat rises to the top, and the defatted liquid can be poured off from the bottom through the spout. A strainer ladle accomplishes the same thing in a different way, acting as a skimmer to collect the fat from the top of the soup or stew while letting the defatted liquid flow back into the pot through the ladle's slotted edge.

SALAD SPINNER The process of cleansing greens—especially sandy ones like spinach—is

enough to put some people off eating salads. A big salad spinner makes quick work of cleaning lettuce, spinach and similar greens; small spinners are just the thing for washing herbs. You place the greens in the slotted interior basket and rinse them under the faucet, then slip the basket into an outer bowl. A crank or a pull cord spins the basket inside the bowl, "centrifuging" the leaves dry without splashing a drop. Store the greens in the spinner until mealtime.

MEASURING CUPS AND SPOONS Careful measuring of ingredients ensures that recipes will come out right (especially in baking, where the recipe is, in a sense, a chemical formula); and a measuring spoon or cup can give you a better idea

of portion sizes. Dry measuring cups come in graduated sizes: For accuracy, overfill the cup a bit, then level the contents with a knife. Clear measures for liquids come in 1-, 2- cup and larger sizes. Pour in the liquid, then check the measurement at eye level (by bending over rather than by lifting the cup). Dry measuring cups and measuring spoons should be deep, with smooth, flat rims for leveling.

SCALE Like measuring cups and spoons, a scale can help you learn to gauge portion sizes for high-fat foods such as meat, cheese and nuts: Once you have an idea of what a 4-ounce burger looks like, you no longer need to weigh the food each time. A scale will help you measure accurately for recipes that call for ingredients by weight, whether you need a 4-ounce fish fillet or a half-pound of potatoes. The best scales have a "tare" setting, which allows you to place a bowl on the platform and then reset to zero before adding the ingredient to be weighed. This function also lets you add one ingredient at a time, weighing each in turn as it goes into the bowl.

NO-STICK POTS AND PANS No-stick cook-ware—greatly improved since its introduction in the 1960s—is an indispensable tool for low-fat cooking. Today's no-stick surfaces, far more durable than the original, can withstand higher

temperatures, and some can be used with metal kitchen utensils (although nylon or wooden tools are kinder to the coating). No-stick finishes are now available on bakeware, broiler pans, woks and appliances such as electric griddles and waffle irons. No-stick cookware may be made of steel, aluminum or even cast-iron, and it pays to invest in good-quality, heavyweight pots and pans, which distribute heat evenly to prevent scorching. A double or triple coating also ensures longer life for the no-stick surface. Even in a no-stick pan, a misting with no-stick spray makes it easier to cook foods that tend to break apart, such as fish fillets or pancakes, but you'll still be using a tiny of fraction of the fat you'd need in a regular pan.

CHEESE GRATER Surveys have shown that people trying to cut down on fat have a very hard time cutting down on cheese. Whether your

favorite is Cheddar, Parmesan or Swiss, it helps to know that the more finely cheese is grated, the further it goes in a recipe or a sandwich—and the more flavor it releases on your tongue, so

you can use less cheese in your favorite dishes. A rotary grater produces very fine shreds of cheese, and works best when the cheese is well chilled.

SHARP KNIVES Literally "cutting the fat" from meat and poultry is much easier when you equip your kitchen with a few good basic knives. The vegetables and fruits that go into healthful meals also need to be sliced, diced and chopped, and good knives speed the job. A chef's knife, with a large, wedge-shaped blade, is a must, as is a small paring knife. Specialized knives for slicing bread, tomatoes or cheese, or for carving, are optional. Fine-quality knives of high-carbon steel (regular or stainless) hold an edge longer and take well to re-sharpening; ingeniously constructed sharpeners make sharpening nearly foolproof. You can also buy state-of-the-art knives that never need sharpening.

Soups & Stews

❧ ❧ ❧

WARMING ONE-DISH MEALS

TO WELCOME THE FAMILY HOME

ON CHILLY NIGHTS

SCALLOP AND POTATO CHOWDER

3 large all-purpose potatoes, peeled and cut into ½-inch chunks

1¾ cups defatted reduced-sodium chicken broth

1 medium onion, diced (about 1 cup)

2 large celery stalks with leaves, thinly sliced (about 1 cup)

½ cup water

1 bay leaf

½ teaspoon freshly ground white pepper

¼ teaspoon dried thyme, crumbled

1 cup 1% low-fat milk

8 ounces sea scallops, rinsed and cut into ½-inch chunks

¼ teaspoon salt

1 tablespoon snipped fresh chives or thinly sliced scallion greens

¼ cup minced red bell peppers for garnish, optional

The word "chowder," usually applied to rich seafood soups, comes from the French word *chaudière,* meaning a large stew pot or caldron. But you don't need a special pot—or any other exotic equipment or ingredients—for this soothing, subtly herbed chowder: A saucepan and a spoon, some fresh vegetables, milk and a half-pound of sea scallops are just about all that's required for a delicious, light dinner that's ready in under an hour.

1 In a large, heavy saucepan, combine the potatoes, broth, onions, celery, water, bay leaf, white pepper and thyme; cover and bring to a boil over high heat. Reduce the heat to medium-low and simmer for 10 minutes, or until the potatoes are fork-tender.

2 Remove the pan from the heat and mash the potatoes slightly to thicken the soup. Stir in the milk.

3 Place the pan of soup over medium heat and bring to a simmer, stirring occasionally. Add the scallops and salt; cook, stirring occasionally, for 3 to 4 minutes, or until the scallops are just firm. Remove from the heat and stir in the chives or scallions. Top the chowder with the red bell peppers, if desired.

Preparation time 20 minutes • **Total time** 40 minutes • **Per serving** 208 calories, 1.8 g. fat (8% of calories), 0.5 g. saturated fat, 21 mg. cholesterol, 572 mg. sodium, 3.2 g. dietary fiber, 124 mg. calcium, 2 mg. iron, 31 mg. vitamin C, 0.1 mg. beta-carotene • **Serves 4**

The freshest chives are those you grow yourself. Potted chives flourish in a sunny window; just snip off the tops as needed.

Preceding pages: Hearty Chicken and Greens Soup (recipe on page 29)

ON THE MENU
Crackers are traditional with chowder, but warm rolls make for an even more inviting meal. Another option: Serve thick slices of bread—perhaps a homemade quick bread flavored with dill and Cheddar.

FOOD FACT
When you're trimming celery stalks, don't toss out the leaves—they are the most flavorful part of the vegetable: This recipe calls for celery stalks with their leaves for just that reason. The leaves add a fresh celery taste to soups and stews (highly preferable to bottled celery powder or celery salt). Crisp celery leaves make a refreshing difference in salads and can also serve as a pretty, edible garnish for a plate or platter. When you do need just the stalks, cut off the tops, wrap them tightly in plastic wrap and freeze them for future use as a seasoning.

MUSHROOM-BARLEY SOUP

1 **ounce dried mushrooms, such as porcini**

1 **cup boiling water**

2 **teaspoons olive oil**

12 **ounces fresh mushrooms, sliced (about 4 cups)**

1 **medium onion, chopped**

¾ **cup thinly sliced carrots**

⅓ **cup thinly sliced shallots or scallions (white parts only)**

2 **garlic cloves, minced**

1¾ **cups defatted reduced-sodium beef broth**

⅓ **cup quick-cooking barley (1½ ounces)**

1 **bay leaf**

¼ **teaspoon freshly ground black pepper**

¼ **teaspoon dill seeds**

1 **tablespoon snipped fresh dill**

Barley is wonderful in soups; you can also cook this flavorful grain as you would rice—steam it, bake it or prepare it as a pilaf—and serve the barley as a side dish or a main-dish casserole.

One of the first crops cultivated by humankind, barley is still an important grain, although American diets are based much more on wheat and rice. Eastern Europeans, on the other hand, have long enjoyed thick barley soups like this one, made with dried mushrooms and dill. For a touch of richness, top each portion of soup with a spoonful of plain yogurt or light sour cream.

1 Place the dried mushrooms in a medium heatproof bowl and pour the boiling water over them. Set aside for 5 minutes, or until the mushrooms have softened.

2 Using a slotted spoon, lift the mushrooms from the liquid, reserving the liquid. Set the mushrooms aside to cool. Strain the reserved liquid through a cheesecloth-lined strainer into a small bowl, leaving behind any sediment. Coarsely chop the softened mushrooms.

3 In a large, heavy saucepan, warm the oil over high heat. Add the dried and fresh mushrooms, the onions, carrots, shallots or scallions and garlic; stir well to coat the vegetables with oil. Reduce the heat to medium-high, cover and cook, stirring occasionally, for 4 to 5 minutes, or until the fresh mushrooms begin to release their liquid.

4 Stir in the reserved mushroom soaking liquid, the broth, barley, bay leaf, black pepper and dill seeds; cover and bring to a boil over high heat. Reduce the heat to medium-low and simmer for 10 to 15 minutes, or until the barley is tender. Just before serving, stir in the fresh dill.

Preparation time 20 minutes • **Total time** 45 minutes • **Per serving** 143 calories, 2.9 g. fat (18% of calories), 0.4 g. saturated fat, 0 mg. cholesterol, 292 mg. sodium, 3.6 g. dietary fiber, 40 mg. calcium, 3 mg. iron, 9 mg. vitamin C, 2 mg. beta-carotene
Serves 4

ON THE MENU
A light meal in itself, the soup also makes a good partner for sandwiches, such as turkey breast on peasant bread with honey-mustard and Romaine lettuce. Offer apples and gingersnaps for dessert.

MARKET AND PANTRY
Shallot heads are formed like garlic, with several cloves individually covered with a thin skin. Their flavor is about midway between onions and garlic. Choose firm, dry shallots free of soft spots or sprouts.

CHICKEN CHILI

1 can (14½ ounces) tomatoes with juice

2 fresh medium tomatoes

1 can (8 ounces) no-salt-added tomato sauce

8 ounces boneless, skinless chicken breasts, cut into chunks

1 large onion, chopped

1 small red bell pepper, diced

1 small green bell pepper, diced

3 tablespoons chili powder

2 garlic cloves, minced

¾ teaspoon ground cumin

½ teaspoon freshly ground black pepper

4 teaspoons olive oil

1 can (16 ounces) red kidney beans, rinsed and drained

1 cup frozen corn kernels

½ cup medium or mild low-sodium salsa

Hot-pepper sauce to taste (optional)

¼ cup chopped fresh cilantro

There are as many ways to make chili as there are chili lovers: with beans, without beans, with chopped meat, with ground meat and with no meat at all. Here is a good basic recipe that you can tailor to your own tastes, adjusting the amounts of chili powder, garlic, salsa and hot-pepper sauce as you like.

1 Coarsely chop the undrained canned tomatoes and the fresh tomatoes in a food processor or by hand; transfer the tomatoes to a large bowl and stir in the tomato sauce.

2 Process the chicken in the food processor until finely chopped. Add the onions, bell peppers, chili powder, garlic, cumin and black pepper, and pulse just until mixed; set aside.

3 In a large, heavy saucepan, warm the oil over high heat until very hot. Add the chicken mixture and sauté for 3 to 4 minutes, or until the chicken turns white.

4 Stir in the tomato mixture, the beans, corn and salsa, and bring the mixture to a boil. Reduce the heat to medium-low, cover the pan and simmer for 10 minutes, or until the flavors are blended. Uncover the pan and simmer for 5 minutes longer.

5 Season the chili with hot-pepper sauce, if using. Ladle the chili into bowls and sprinkle with the cilantro.

Preparation time 20 minutes • **Total time** 40 minutes • **Per serving** 329 calories, 8 g. fat (22% of calories), 0.9 g. saturated fat, 33 mg. cholesterol, 426 mg. sodium, 11.2 g. dietary fiber, 101 mg. calcium, 4 mg. iron, 88 mg. vitamin C, 3 mg. beta-carotene • **Serves 4**

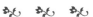

MARKET AND PANTRY
Buying tomatoes out of season can be a risky proposition. Most are picked green so they'll survive shipping, and of these, the majority will ripen, but some—picked a bit too early—will never soften, turn red or develop any flavor. With that in mind, your best bet is to choose the reddest (or pinkest) tomatoes available and to look for heavy specimens that yield slightly when pressed between your hands. Ripen the tomatoes at room temperature for a few days; placing them in a paper bag with an apple will speed the natural ripening process. Never refrigerate tomatoes—it destroys both their flavor and texture.

New-Fashioned Beef Stew

4 small red potatoes

1 medium turnip

1 medium parsnip

1 cup peeled pearl onions

3 medium carrots

1 cup drained canned tomatoes

1¾ cups defatted reduced-sodium beef broth

1 tablespoon red wine vinegar

2 garlic cloves, crushed

1 bay leaf

½ teaspoon dried thyme, crumbled

½ teaspoon freshly ground black pepper

12 ounces lean, trimmed beef top round or sirloin, cut into ½-inch cubes

1 tablespoon all-purpose flour

1 tablespoon olive oil

Heating up a can of beef stew is one way of putting a quick hot meal on the table, but it's not the only alternative—and certainly not the best one—to spending hours over the stove. This chunky beef-and-vegetable stew is prepared in a streamlined fashion—the meat is quickly sautéed, then added to the already cooked vegetables.

1 Cut each potato into 6 wedges. Peel the turnip and cut it into chunks. Peel the parsnip and cut it into chunks. Peel the onions. Peel the carrots and cut them into chunks.

2 In a large, heavy saucepan, combine the potatoes, turnips, parsnips, onions, carrots, tomatoes, broth, vinegar, half the garlic, the bay leaf, ¼ teaspoon of the thyme and ¼ teaspoon of the black pepper. Break up the tomatoes with the edge of a spoon. Cover and bring to a boil over high heat. Reduce the heat to medium and simmer for 25 minutes, or until the vegetables are just tender.

3 Meanwhile, toss the beef cubes with the remaining garlic and the remaining ¼ teaspoon each thyme and black pepper. Dredge the seasoned beef cubes with the flour.

4 In a large, heavy skillet, warm the oil over high heat until very hot but not smoking. Add the beef and sauté for 5 minutes, or until the beef is browned on the outside and medium-rare on the inside.

5 Add the beef to the vegetables, reduce the heat to medium-low and simmer for 5 minutes, or until the vegetables are fully tender and the flavors are blended.

Preparation time 20 minutes • **Total time** 45 minutes • **Per serving** 335 calories, 6.9 g. fat (18% of calories), 1.5 g. saturated fat, 49 mg. cholesterol, 469 mg. sodium, 6.9 g. dietary fiber, 72 mg. calcium, 4 mg. iron, 47 mg. vitamin C, 9 mg. beta-carotene
Serves 4

Carrot-size parsnips (8 to 9 inches long) are likely to be tender throughout. Larger parsnips, which may be overmature, tend to have tough, woody cores that will need to be removed.

BLACK BEAN SOUP

2 cans (19 ounces each) black beans, rinsed and drained

1¾ cups defatted low-sodium chicken broth

1 cup water

1 teaspoon ground cumin

¼ teaspoon dried oregano

¼ teaspoon freshly ground black pepper

Large pinch of ground red pepper

1 teaspoon olive oil

½ large red bell pepper, slivered

½ large green bell pepper, slivered

½ teaspoon grated lemon zest

Bean soups, from sustaining Yankee bean to savory Italian minestrone, find favor all over the world. If you'd like to make this soup with dried black beans, place 1 pound of beans in a large pot with cold water to cover; refrigerate overnight. Drain the beans, cover with fresh water, and simmer for 1¼ hours, or until tender. You'll have enough for this recipe, plus leftovers for other dishes.

1 In a large, heavy saucepan, combine the beans, broth, water, cumin, oregano, black pepper and ground red pepper. Cover and bring to a boil over high heat. Reduce the heat to low and simmer, stirring once or twice, for 15 minutes, or until the flavors are blended.

2 Meanwhile, in a small no-stick skillet, warm the oil over medium-high heat. Add the bell peppers, reduce the heat to medium and sauté for 4 to 6 minutes, or until tender.

3 Ladle half of the soup into a food processor or blender and process until puréed (work in batches if necessary). Return the purée to the pan; add the lemon zest.

4 Ladle the soup into bowls and top each serving with some of the sautéed bell peppers.

Preparation time 15 minutes • **Total time** 35 minutes • **Per serving** 182 calories, 3.1 g. fat (15% of calories), 0.4 g. saturated fat, 0 mg. cholesterol, 460 mg. sodium, 7.8 g. dietary fiber, 62 mg. calcium, 4 mg. iron, 38 mg. vitamin C, 0.3 mg. beta-carotene • **Serves 4**

❧ ❧ ❧

To soak dried beans, place them in a pot or bowl and add cold water to cover.

After soaking, simmer the beans in fresh water, skimming the foam as they cook.

HEARTY CHICKEN AND GREENS SOUP

1 medium leek

2 cups water

1¾ cups defatted reduced-sodium chicken broth

8 ounces boneless, skinless chicken breasts, cut crosswise into ½-inch-thick strips

1 cup frozen chopped leaf spinach

2 large carrots, sliced

2 garlic cloves, minced

½ teaspoon dried thyme, crumbled

¼ teaspoon salt

¼ teaspoon freshly ground black pepper

3 ounces thin egg noodles

2 tablespoons chopped fresh Italian parsley

Chicken soup may really be good for a cold (scientific research has shown that its steamy heat does help clear your head). Medicinal properties aside, however, a bowl of this home-made soup, brimming with chunks of chicken, vegetables and egg noodles, seems to make everyone feel better, especially on a chilly autumn or winter evening.

1 Halve the leek lengthwise and rinse each half well under cold running water. Cut the leek halves crosswise into ½-inch pieces.

2 In a large, heavy saucepan, combine the leeks, water, broth, chicken strips, spinach, carrots, garlic, thyme, salt and black pepper. Cover and bring to a boil over high heat. Reduce the heat to low and simmer for 8 minutes.

3 Stir in the noodles, increase the heat to medium-high and return to a boil. Reduce the heat to medium-low, cover and simmer, stirring occasionally, for 4 to 6 minutes, or until the noodles, vegetables and chicken are tender.

4 Remove the pan from the heat and stir in the parsley.

Preparation time 10 minutes • **Total time** 35 minutes • **Per serving** 217 calories, 2.5 g. fat (10% of calories), 0.4 g. saturated fat, 53 mg. cholesterol, 523 mg. sodium, 3.9 g. dietary fiber, 121 mg. calcium, 4 mg. iron, 26 mg. vitamin C, 11 mg. beta-carotene • **Serves 4**

❧ ❧ ❧

To clean leeks, first cut off the coarse parts of the green tops (leave on the tender green parts for this recipe).

Sand can get caught between the layers of the leek; splitting the leek lengthwise makes it easier to wash the sand away.

Hold the split leeks under cold running water, fanning the layers to release any dirt. Wash the leaves separately.

LAMB AND POTATO STEW WITH PEAS

1½ pounds new red potatoes, thinly sliced

1¾ cups defatted reduced-sodium chicken broth

1 large onion, halved and thinly sliced

3 garlic cloves, crushed

½ teaspoon freshly ground black pepper

½ teaspoon dried rosemary, crushed

12 ounces lean, boneless trimmed lamb steak, cut into ½-inch cubes

⅛ teaspoon salt

1 tablespoon all-purpose flour

1 tablespoon olive oil

1 cup frozen peas

2 tablespoons chopped fresh Italian parsley

Hearty Irish stew, a classic of country cooking, relies on starchy potatoes to thicken the mixture as it cooks. The French equivalent, *navarin printanier*, is somewhat more delicate, made with spring vegetables and new potatoes that have been painstakingly trimmed into uniform ovals. This version is on the lighter side: The sliced new potatoes hold their shape rather than falling apart, and green peas and parsley add a note of spring freshness.

1 In a large, heavy saucepan, combine the potatoes, broth, onions, half of the garlic, ¼ teaspoon of the black pepper and ¼ teaspoon of the rosemary. Cover and bring to a boil over high heat. Reduce the heat to medium-low and simmer, stirring occasionally, for 15 minutes, or until the potatoes are fork-tender.

2 While the potatoes are cooking, place the lamb cubes in a medium bowl. Add the remaining garlic, black pepper and rosemary, and the salt, and toss until the lamb is coated with the seasonings. Sprinkle in the flour and toss the lamb cubes until they are coated with flour.

3 In a large, heavy no-stick skillet, warm the oil over high heat until very hot. Add the lamb cubes and sauté for 5 minutes, or until the lamb is medium-rare.

4 Add the lamb to the potato mixture, then stir in the peas, cover, and simmer for 2 to 3 minutes longer, or until the peas are heated through. Sprinkle the stew with the parsley and serve.

Preparation time 15 minutes • **Total time** 45 minutes • **Per serving** 361 calories, 10.2 g. fat (25% of calories), 2.5 g. saturated fat, 56 mg. cholesterol, 465 mg. sodium, 5.3 g. dietary fiber, 42 mg. calcium, 4 mg. iron, 39 mg. vitamin C, 0.2 mg. beta-carotene • **Serves 4**

New potatoes—freshly harvested ones that have not been stored—have a lower starch content than mature potatoes. They cook quickly and have a slightly sweet flavor.

MARKET AND PANTRY
Look for unusual potato varieties at gourmet groceries and farmers' markets. The small, pink Rose Fir has joined the Red LaSoda and Red Pontiac as a favorite red potato. Yukon Gold and Finnish Yellow Wax potatoes are deep yellow within: The butter-hued flesh of these varieties can be a healthful palate-fooler, convincing people to skip the butter they would otherwise add. Among the most novel potatoes are the Blue Carib and the All Blue; their purple-blue skin and dark blue flesh add a jolt of color to the dinner plate.

Poultry, Fish & Meat

❧ ❧ ❧

SERVE CHICKEN OR CHOPS,

SNAPPER OR SCALLOPS—AND

TAKE A HEALTHIER LOOK AT THE

HEARTIEST OF MEALS

ROSEMARY-ORANGE CHICKEN ON SPINACH

1 large navel orange

2–3 tablespoons orange juice

1 tablespoon olive oil

2 teaspoons balsamic vinegar

½ teaspoon dried rosemary, crumbled

¼ teaspoon light brown sugar

Pinch of crushed red pepper flakes

1 pound thin-sliced chicken cutlets

¼ teaspoon freshly ground black pepper

¼ teaspoon salt

1 pound washed spinach, tough stems removed

The novel interplay of seasonings in this dish will surprise and intrigue anyone who ever thought chicken was boring: There's the freshness of citrus, the mellow tang of balsamic vinegar, the pungency of rosemary and the bite of black and red pepper. If you can't find balsamic vinegar, which is carefully aged to produce its unique flavor, substitute a mild red wine vinegar.

1 Grate ½ teaspoon of zest from the orange; set the zest aside. Using a sharp paring knife, peel the orange, removing all of the white pith. Working over a bowl, cut between the membranes to divide the orange into sections. Squeeze the membranes between your fingers to release all the juice, then discard them. Pour all the juice from the bowl into a measuring cup, then add enough additional orange juice to measure ⅓ cup.

2 Add the orange zest, 1 teaspoon of the oil, the vinegar, ¼ teaspoon of the rosemary, the sugar and red pepper flakes to the orange juice, and whisk until blended; set aside.

3 Sprinkle the chicken with the remaining ¼ teaspoon rosemary, the black pepper and salt. In a large no-stick skillet, warm the remaining 2 teaspoons oil over high heat until hot but not smoking. Working in batches, if necessary, add the chicken and sauté for 2 to 3 minutes per side, or until lightly browned and cooked through. Transfer the chicken to a platter and cover loosely with a sheet of foil.

4 Add the spinach to the skillet and stir-fry over high heat for 1 to 2 minutes, or just until the spinach is wilted.

5 Arrange the spinach around the chicken on the platter and place the orange sections on the chicken.

6 Whisk the dressing briefly to reblend it, then pour the dressing over the chicken and spinach.

Preparation time 25 minutes • **Total time** 35 minutes • **Per serving** 199 calories, 5.1 g. fat (23% of calories), 1 g. saturated fat, 66 mg. cholesterol, 274 mg. sodium, 3.2 g. dietary fiber, 115 mg. calcium, 3 mg. iron, 54 mg. vitamin C, 3.4 mg. beta-carotene • **Serves 4**

❧ ❧ ❧

Preceding pages: Scallop Sauté with Vegetables (recipe on page 59)

SWEET-AND-SOUR PORK CHOPS

¼ cup reduced-sodium ketchup

¼ cup frozen pineapple juice concentrate

3 tablespoons water

2 teaspoons cornstarch

2 teaspoons reduced-sodium soy sauce

¼ teaspoon crushed red pepper flakes

¼ teaspoon dry mustard

2 garlic cloves

1 slice (¼-inch-thick) peeled fresh ginger

1 large red bell pepper, cut into chunks

1 medium onion, cut into ¼-inch dice

1 can (8¼ ounces) juice-packed pineapple rings, drained and cut in half

1½ pounds well-trimmed thin-sliced pork chops (4 chops)

1 tablespoon chopped fresh cilantro (optional)

Pork goes particularly well with piquant sauces such as the sweet-and-sour basting mixture used here. Although the flavors are inspired by Chinese cuisine, the ingredients are all readily available in supermarkets. Reduced-sodium soy sauce contains about one-third less sodium than regular soy sauce—it isn't a low-sodium condiment, but is quite an improvement over the original.

1 Preheat the oven to 450°. Spray a roasting pan or the bottom of a broiler pan with no-stick spray.

2 Combine the ketchup, pineapple juice concentrate, water, cornstarch, soy sauce, crushed red pepper and mustard in a food processor. With the machine running, drop the garlic, then the ginger, through the feed tube and process until puréed.

3 Place the bell peppers, onions and pineapple in the prepared pan and toss with about 3 tablespoons of the ketchup mixture; spread into an even layer. Coat both sides of the chops with the remaining ketchup mixture and place the chops on top of the vegetables and pineapple.

4 Bake for 20 to 25 minutes, or until the vegetables are tender and the pork chops are cooked medium. Transfer the chops, vegetables and pineapple to a heated platter and sprinkle with the cilantro, if using.

Preparation time 20 minutes • **Total time** 45 minutes • **Per serving** 281 calories, 6.6 g. fat (21% of calories), 2 g. saturated fat, 77 mg. cholesterol, 294 mg. sodium, 1.5 g. dietary fiber, 62 mg. calcium, 2 mg. iron, 65 mg. vitamin C, 1 mg. beta-carotene • **Serves 4**

ON THE MENU
Serve this generous entrée with rice, cooked while the pork chops are in the oven. Underscore the Asian theme with almond cookies and tea for dessert.

NUTRITION NOTE
Improved methods of breeding and raising pigs have lowered the fat content of pork by more than 30 percent over the past ten years. Pork has always been an excellent source of B vitamins, especially thiamin. Like other types of meat, pork is a good source of iron.

MARKET AND PANTRY
Fresh ginger should be firm, its paper-thin tan skin tight and glossy. Avoid ginger roots that feel soft and flabby, or those with dull, wrinkled skin.

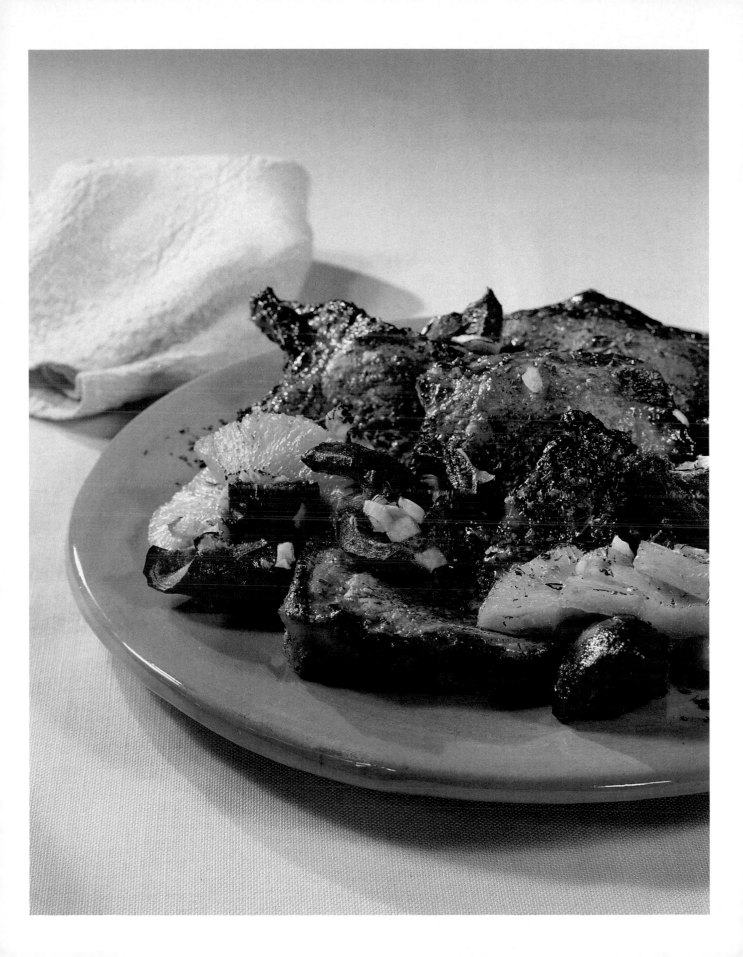

FISH FINGERS WITH SPICY SAUCE

Fish Fingers

1 pound lemon sole, scrod or tilefish fillets, about 1 inch thick

1 tablespoon fresh lime juice

⅛ teaspoon salt

⅛ teaspoon freshly ground black pepper

⅛ teaspoon ground red pepper (optional)

¾ cup unseasoned dry breadcrumbs

1 large egg white

2 teaspoons olive oil

Spicy Sauce

½ cup nonfat sour cream

¼ cup medium or mild salsa

1 tablespoon chopped fresh cilantro

1 teaspoon fresh lime juice

Lime wedges, for garnish (optional)

Children love fish sticks—in fact, some turn up their noses at just about everything else. Unfortunately, a serving of fish sticks can have as much as 20 grams of fat, and some brands are also very high in sodium. The solution to this dietary dilemma is homemade fish fingers, put together quickly from fresh ingredients. The dipping sauce is a tangy blend of salsa and sour cream.

1 Preheat the oven to 400°. Spray a jelly-roll pan with no-stick spray.

2 To make the fish fingers: Cut the fish into 2-inch-long strips. Drizzle the fish with the lime juice and season with the salt and black pepper and the red pepper, if using.

3 Spread the breadcrumbs on a plate. In a medium bowl, lightly beat the egg white; add the fish and toss to coat. One piece at a time, roll the fish strips in the breadcrumbs to coat completely. Arrange the fish strips in a single layer in the prepared pan and drizzle them evenly with the oil.

4 Bake the fish fingers for 10 to 15 minutes, or until the crumb crust is lightly browned and the fish flakes when tested with a fork.

5 While the fish is cooking, make the sauce: In a small bowl, stir together the sour cream, salsa, cilantro and lime juice. Serve the fish with the sauce, garnished with lime wedges, if desired.

Preparation time 20 minutes • **Total time** 35 minutes • **Per serving** 220 calories, 4.8 g. fat (20% of calories), 1 g. saturated fat, 55 mg. cholesterol, 424 mg. sodium, 1 g. dietary fiber, 98 mg. calcium, 1 mg. iron, 12 mg. vitamin C, 0 mg. beta-carotene
Serves 4

FOR A CHANGE
For a less spicy dish, leave out the ground red pepper and choose a mild salsa.

KITCHEN TIPS
The fish fillets should be fairly thick to produce finger-size pieces. If you're using thin sole fillets, cut them into 2-inch-wide pieces; cut thicker scrod or tilefish fillets into 1-inch-wide pieces.

ON THE MENU
Accompany the fish fingers with carrot, celery and cucumber sticks (you can dip them in the sauce); try sherbet "floats" for a child-pleasing dessert.

COUNTRY CAPTAIN CHICKEN

2 garlic cloves, crushed

1 tablespoon curry powder or more to taste

2 teaspoons olive oil

1 teaspoon water

½ teaspoon dried thyme, crumbled

⅛ teaspoon freshly ground black pepper

2 pounds bone-in skinless chicken breast halves

1 large onion, sliced

1 large green bell pepper, cut into thin strips

2 large celery stalks with leaves, sliced

⅓ cup defatted chicken broth

1 can (14½ ounces) whole tomatoes, drained and coarsely chopped

3 tablespoons raisins

¼ cup chopped fresh cilantro (optional)

The route by which this dish came to America from India is uncertain, but tradition has it that the recipe was brought to Savannah by spice traders; indeed, Country Captain is still very popular in the South. The primary seasoning is curry powder, which may include turmeric, cardamom, coriander, cumin, ginger, mustard, pepper, cloves and fenugreek. Curry powders vary in strength, so let your taste be your guide as to how much you use. As befits a dish of Indian origin, Country Captain is usually served with rice.

1 Preheat the oven to 425°. Spray a 9 x 13-inch baking dish with no stick spray.

2 In a cup, mix the garlic, 2 teaspoons of the curry powder, the oil, water, thyme and ground black pepper. Rub the mixture over both sides of the chicken breasts and place the chicken, bone side down, in the prepared baking dish. Bake for 15 minutes, or until the chicken is light golden brown.

3 Meanwhile, in a large, heavy saucepan, combine the onions, bell peppers, celery, broth and the remaining 1 teaspoon curry powder; cover and bring to a boil over high heat. Reduce the heat to medium, and simmer for 5 minutes, or until the vegetables are crisp-tender.

4 Uncover the pan, increase the heat to high and stir in the tomatoes and raisins; bring just to a boil. Taste the mixture and add more curry powder, if desired. Spoon the vegetable mixture evenly over the chicken, mixing it with any juices in the baking dish.

5 Cover the dish with a sheet of foil and bake for 10 minutes longer, or until the chicken is cooked through and the juices are bubbly. Divide the vegetables among 4 plates and top each portion with a chicken breast. Sprinkle with the cilantro, if desired.

Preparation time 15 minutes • **Total time** 50 minutes • **Per serving** 297 calories, 5.4 g. fat (16% of calories), 1 g. saturated fat, 101 mg. cholesterol, 388 mg. sodium, 3.4 g. dietary fiber, 88 mg. calcium, 3 mg. iron, 46 mg. vitamin C, 0.5 mg. beta-carotene • **Serves 4**

ROSEMARY-FENNEL LAMB CHOPS

1 teaspoon dried rosemary

1 teaspoon dried thyme

½ teaspoon garlic powder

¼ teaspoon fennel seeds

¼ teaspoon freshly ground black pepper

¼ teaspoon salt

1½ pounds rib lamb chops (4 chops)

Rubbing freshly ground herbs and spices into meat or poultry accomplishes the same purpose as marinating, but does it more quickly and produces a more intense flavor. You have a number of options for grinding the spices: A mortar and pestle is traditional for this job, and small but sturdy marble or porcelain sets are inexpensive. Handheld electric coffee mills (also sold as spice mills) are perfect for grinding spices. It's best, however, not to use the same mill for coffee and spices: Both have pervasive aromas and you may end up with coffee-flavored spices or spice-scented coffee.

1 In a clean coffee or spice mill, or in a mortar and pestle, grind the rosemary, thyme, garlic powder, fennel seeds, pepper and salt to a fine powder. Rub the spice mixture over both sides of the lamb chops and place them on a plate; cover and let stand at room temperature for 15 minutes.

2 Preheat the broiler. Place the chops on a broiler-pan rack and broil 4 to 5 inches from the heat source for 6 to 7 minutes, then turn the chops and cook for 5 to 6 minutes for medium-rare (the cooking time will depend on the thickness of the chops).

A small stone or ceramic mortar and pestle is an old-fashioned but highly efficient device for crushing herbs and spices.

Preparation time 10 minutes • **Total time** 40 minutes • **Per serving** 132 calories, 7.1 g. fat (49% of calories), 2.5 g. saturated fat, 50 mg. cholesterol, 182 mg. sodium, 0 g. dietary fiber, 22 mg. calcium, 2 mg. iron, 0 mg. vitamin C, 0 mg. beta-carotene
Serves 4

ON THE MENU
Complement the full-flavored lamb with a salad of tart-bitter greens such as chicory, arugula or mizuna (Japanese mustard greens). Rice pilaf, orzo (rice-shaped pasta) or couscous provides a fine foil for the meat's richness.

HEAD START
Grind the herbs and spices in advance and store them in a small jar with a tight-fitting lid or in a twist of plastic wrap.

MARKET AND PANTRY
Good-quality fresh lamb is pinkish (not dark red) and firm. Lamb chops will keep for two to four days in the refrigerator.

FOOD FACT
Fennel seeds come from common fennel, close kin to Florence fennel, of which we eat the root and stalks. (Both plants are related to the wildflower Queen Anne's lace.) Common fennel yields flat, greenish-tan seeds with a mild anise flavor.

SNAPPER WITH MUSTARD-DILL TOPPING

2 tablespoons plus 1 teaspoon reduced-calorie mayonnaise

1 tablespoon snipped fresh dill

1 tablespoon grated Parmesan cheese

2 teaspoons fresh lemon juice

1½ teaspoons coarse Dijon mustard

¼ teaspoon freshly ground black pepper

1 pound red snapper or striped bass fillets, cut into 4 pieces

Lemon wedges and dill sprigs, for garnish (optional)

Delectable red snapper is a warm-water fish that is caught in the Atlantic along the southeast coast of the United States and also in the Gulf of Mexico. Its skin is a shimmering pink or red, depending on the size of the fish. Other species of snapper, such as the gray, appear in American markets, but red snapper, even when sold as fillets, usually has its skin left on to identify it. Striped bass, which may be substituted for snapper, is a similarly lean, flavorful fish.

1 Preheat the broiler. Spray a broiler-pan rack with no-stick spray.

2 In a small bowl, mix the mayonnaise, snipped dill, Parmesan, lemon juice, mustard and pepper.

3 Place the fish fillets on the prepared broiler-pan rack and spread the mayonnaise mixture evenly over them.

4 Broil 4 to 6 inches from the heat for 6 to 8 minutes, or until the topping is well browned in spots and the fish just flakes when tested with a knife.

5 Serve the fish garnished with lemon wedges and dill sprigs, if desired.

Preparation time 5 minutes • **Total time** 15 minutes • **Per serving** 148 calories, 4.6 g. fat (28% of calories), 1.1 g. saturated fat, 46 mg. cholesterol, 200 mg. sodium, 0 g. dietary fiber, 58 mg. calcium, 0 mg. iron, 1 mg. vitamin C, 0.1 mg. beta carotene
Serves 4

The "Canadian rule" can help you gauge cooking time for fish (see right).

KITCHEN TIPS
Fish cooks very quickly and can overcook in a matter of minutes. When following a recipe, test the fish a little before the suggested cooking time has elapsed. If you're not using a recipe, the so-called Canadian rule (developed by the Canadian Department of Fisheries) can serve as a rough guide for baking or broiling: Measure the fish at its thickest point, then allow 10 minutes of cooking time for each inch of thickness. Even with this general guideline, it's important to test the fish for doneness. Using a sharp knife, make a small cut in the thickest part of the fish: The flesh should separate along its natural grain, but should still look very moist and just slightly translucent, as it will continue to cook from retained heat after you remove it from the oven. The description of fish "flaking" when tested does not mean that it should fall apart into flakes when you cut into it. If cooked to this point, the fish will be overdone and dry.

MOZZARELLA MEATBALLS

- 12 ounces lean, trimmed beef top round
- 1 large egg white
- 2 tablespoons unseasoned dry breadcrumbs
- 1 tablespoon grated Parmesan cheese
- 1 tablespoon chopped fresh Italian parsley
- 1 garlic clove, crushed
- 1½ teaspoons dried Italian herb seasoning
- ¼ teaspoon freshly ground black pepper
- ⅛ teaspoon salt
- 2 cans (8 ounces each) no-salt-added tomato sauce
- 1 medium zucchini, thinly sliced crosswise
- 2½ ounces part-skim mozzarella cheese, shredded

This knife-and-fork version of an Italian meatball hero demands delicious, crusty bread on the side; you could also serve the meatballs and vegetables atop a thick, toasted slice of Italian or French bread. One way to form the beef mixture into equal-size meatballs is to shape it into an 8-inch log, then cut it crosswise into 16 equal slices and roll them, with moistened hands, into balls.

1 Preheat the broiler. Spray a broiler-pan rack with no-stick spray.

2 Cut the beef into cubes and process it in a food processor until finely chopped. Add the egg white, breadcrumbs, Parmesan, parsley, garlic, 1 teaspoon of the Italian seasoning, the pepper and salt to the processor; process briefly to mix.

3 Shape the mixture into 16 meatballs, using a scant tablespoon for each. Arrange the meatballs on the prepared broiler-pan rack and broil 5 to 6 inches from the heat for 5 to 6 minutes, or until the meatballs are no longer pink in the center. Remove from the broiler.

4 Combine the tomato sauce, zucchini and remaining ½ teaspoon Italian seasoning in a deep medium skillet; bring to a boil over high heat, stirring frequently. Add the meatballs and return to a boil. Reduce the heat to medium-low, cover and simmer for 5 minutes to blend the flavors.

5 Sprinkle the meatballs with the mozzarella; cover and simmer for 1 to 2 minutes longer, or until the cheese is melted.

Preparation time 25 minutes • **Total time** 45 minutes • **Per serving** 229 calories, 7 g. fat (28% of calories), 3.1 g. saturated fat, 60 mg. cholesterol, 300 mg. sodium, 2.1 g. dietary fiber, 156 mg. calcium, 3 mg. iron, 23 mg. vitamin C, 1 mg. beta-carotene • **Serves 4**

Shape the meatballs lightly with your fingers; if the mixture is compacted too firmly, the meatballs will be tough.

KITCHEN TIP

The slicing slot on a grater—if it is sharp—can be used to slice the zucchini. Otherwise, try a food processor, or slice the zucchini with a good, heavy chef's knife—an indispensable kitchen tool.

MARKET AND PANTRY

Italian herb seasoning is an herb-and-spice blend that helps you achieve just the right flavor balance. It usually consists of oregano, basil, marjoram, thyme, summer savory, rosemary and sage.

BAKED CHICKEN OREGANATA

1 **pound boneless, skinless chicken thighs, well trimmed**

1 **tablespoon lemon juice**

2 **garlic cloves, crushed**

1 **teaspoon dried oregano, crumbled**

½ **teaspoon freshly ground black pepper**

¼ **teaspoon dried mint, crumbled**

⅛ **teaspoon salt**

¼ **cup unseasoned dry breadcrumbs**

2 **tablespoons grated Parmesan cheese**

2 **large tomatoes (about 1 pound), each cut into 10 wedges**

1 **teaspoon olive oil**

A thick, crunchy coat of Parmesan- and herb-flavored bread-crumbs keeps these skinless chicken thighs juicy, as do the tomatoes baked alongside. The dark meat of poultry is higher in fat than the white meat, but you can reduce the overall fat content of a dish made with chicken thighs by removing the skin and trimming all visible fat before cooking.

1 Preheat the oven to 450°. Coat a 9 x 13-inch baking dish with no-stick spray.

2 Place the chicken in a medium bowl with the lemon juice and garlic, and toss to combine.

3 In a cup, stir together the oregano, pepper, mint and salt. Place the breadcrumbs in a small bowl and stir in the Parmesan and half of the oregano mixture.

4 Scatter the breadcrumbs over the chicken; toss to coat the chicken with the crumbs. Place the chicken in the prepared baking dish and arrange the tomatoes around the chicken. Drizzle the oil over the chicken and sprinkle the remaining herb mixture over the tomatoes.

5 Bake for 25 to 30 minutes, or until chicken is cooked through and the tomatoes are soft and juicy. Serve the chicken and tomatoes topped with the pan juices.

Preparation time 15 minutes • **Total time** 45 minutes • **Per serving** 214 calories, 7.3 g. fat (31% of calories), 1.9 g. saturated fat, 96 mg. cholesterol, 282 mg. sodium, 1.8 g. dietary fiber, 77 mg. calcium, 2 mg. iron, 27 mg. vitamin C, 0.4 mg. beta-carotene • **Serves 4**

ON THE MENU
Serve the chicken with spinach fettuccine or a rice pilaf, along with a salad of cucumbers and scallions.

KITCHEN TIPS
It's easy to make your own dry bread-crumbs. Lay bread slices on a baking sheet and bake at 300° until dry and very lightly browned. After the bread cools, tear it into pieces and process into crumbs in a food processor or blender: One slice of bread yields about ⅓ cup of crumbs. The dry crumbs, tightly sealed in a plastic bag, can be refrigerated for a week or frozen for about six months.

STEAK WITH MANY PEPPERS

12 ounces well-trimmed boneless
    sirloin steak

 2 garlic cloves, minced

¾ teaspoon coarsely ground black
    pepper

¼ teaspoon salt

 1 tablespoon balsamic vinegar

 1 teaspoon extra-virgin olive oil

 1 small red bell pepper, thinly
    sliced

 1 small green bell pepper, thinly
    sliced

 1 small yellow bell pepper, thinly
    sliced

 1 medium onion, halved and cut
    into thin wedges

 1 large ripe tomato, cut into thin
    wedges

 1 tablespoon defatted chicken
    broth or water

 1 tablespoon chopped fresh
    oregano or 2 tablespoons
    chopped fresh Italian parsley

You needn't give a moment's thought to garnishing this dish—the vivid colors of the bell peppers and tomatoes make it quite irresistible without any extra fuss or flourishes. To balance this entrée—in which most of the calories come from the meat—serve it with bread, rice or potatoes; the addition of carbohydrates will drop the percentage of calories from fat in the meal well below its current 32 percent.

1 Preheat the broiler. Spray a broiler-pan rack with no-stick spray.

2 Rub both sides of the steak with the garlic, pepper and ⅛ teaspoon of the salt; place the steak on the prepared rack and drizzle it with 1 teaspoon of the vinegar. Broil 5 to 6 inches from the heat for about 5 minutes, then turn the steak and drizzle the second side with another teaspoon of vinegar. Broil for 4 to 5 minutes longer for medium-rare. Transfer the steak to a warmed platter, cover loosely with foil and let stand for 5 minutes.

3 While the steak is cooking, in a deep, medium no-stick skillet, warm the oil over high heat until hot. Add the bell peppers and onions, and toss to coat them with oil; cook, stirring, for 1 minute. Reduce the heat to medium-high, add the tomatoes and broth or water, and toss to combine. Cover and cook, stirring frequently, for 8 to 10 minutes, or until the vegetables are tender.

4 Uncover the skillet and add the remaining 1 teaspoon vinegar, ⅛ teaspoon salt and any juices that have collected on the steak platter; simmer for 1 minute. Remove from the heat and stir in the oregano or parsley.

5 Carve the steak into thin slices and arrange on the platter. Spoon the vegetables and pan juices around the steak.

Preparation time 10 minutes • **Total time** 35 minutes • **Per serving** 177 calories, 6.3 g. fat (32% of calories), 2 g. saturated fat, 57 mg. cholesterol, 199 mg. sodium, 1.9 g. dietary fiber, 31 mg. calcium, 3 mg. iron, 63 mg. vitamin C, 0.8 mg. beta-carotene • **Serves 4**

CHICKEN LEGS WITH CHILI BEANS

1¼ **pounds skinned chicken legs, drumsticks and thighs cut apart**

3 **garlic cloves, crushed**

2 **tablespoons chili powder**

1 **teaspoon olive oil**

1 **medium onion, chopped**

1 **medium green bell pepper, diced**

2 **tablespoons defatted chicken broth**

2 **teaspoons diced seeded, pickled jalapeño peppers**

1 **can (16 ounces) red kidney beans, rinsed and drained**

1 **can (14½ ounces) no-salt-added stewed tomatoes**

This hearty supper gets its tongue-tingling kick from chili powder and pickled jalapeños. Chili powder is a blend of ground dried chilies with other seasonings, which may include garlic, cumin, coriander, cloves, oregano, thyme and salt. Chili powder is sold in different "heats" and comes in salt-free versions, too. Not just for chili, the spice blend can also be added to soups and salad dressings.

1 Preheat the oven to 425°. Coat a jelly-roll pan with no-stick spray.

2 Place the chicken pieces in the pan and rub them with the garlic and 1 tablespoon of the chili powder. Drizzle with the oil. Bake for 20 to 25 minutes, or until the chicken is no longer pink near the bone.

3 Meanwhile, in a large no-stick skillet, combine the onions, bell peppers and broth, and sauté for 4 to 6 minutes, or until the vegetables are tender. Stir in the jalapeños and the remaining 1 tablespoon chili powder, and cook, stirring constantly, for 30 seconds.

4 Add the beans and stewed tomatoes, and bring to a simmer. Reduce the heat to low, cover and simmer, stirring occasionally, for 10 minutes. Serve the chili beans with the chicken.

Preparation time 15 minutes • **Total time** 45 minutes • **Per serving** 272 calories, 6.6 g. fat (22% of calories), 1.2 g. saturated fat, 77 mg. cholesterol, 333 mg. sodium, 9.1 g. dietary fiber, 95 mg. calcium, 4 mg. iron, 40 mg. vitamin C, 1.2 mg. beta-carotene • **Serves 4**

To cut apart the chicken thigh and leg, first cut through the joint from the top.

Then turn the thigh over, skin side down, and cut through the joint.

BEEF AND CORN SKILLET

½ cup raw converted white rice

1 cup water

8 ounces lean, well-trimmed beef top round

1 tablespoon chili powder

2 teaspoons olive oil

⅛ teaspoon salt

1 large onion, thinly sliced

1 medium green bell pepper, thinly sliced

1½ cups crushed canned tomatoes

1 cup frozen corn kernels

Two favorite ethnic cuisines come together in this stir-fry with a Tex-Mex twist. Although stir-frying is an Asian technique, this quick cooking method can be adapted to many other dishes. You can flavor stir-fried vegetables with Indian curry spices, toss stir-fried chicken strips with pasta and Italian seasoning or try this chili-sauced medley of beef, corn and bell peppers served over rice.

1 In a heavy, medium saucepan, combine the rice and water; bring to a boil over high heat. Reduce the heat to low, cover and simmer for 20 minutes, or until the rice is tender and the liquid has been absorbed.

2 While the rice is cooking, cut the beef into very thin strips and sprinkle with the chili powder; toss to coat.

3 In a large no-stick skillet, warm the oil over high heat until very hot. Add the beef and stir-fry for 2 to 3 minutes, or until the beef is no longer pink. Sprinkle the beef with the salt.

4 Add the onions and bell peppers; toss well to mix with the beef and the pan juices. Reduce the heat to medium-high and stir-fry for 4 to 5 minutes, or until the vegetables are tender and the beef is cooked through.

5 Stir in the tomatoes and corn; bring the mixture to a boil. Reduce the heat to medium and simmer for 3 to 4 minutes, or until the corn is hot. Serve the beef mixture over the hot rice.

Preparation time 10 minutes • **Total time** 40 minutes • **Per serving** 269 calories, 5.3 g. fat (18% of calories), 1.1 g. saturated fat, 32 mg. cholesterol, 269 mg. sodium, 4 g. dietary fiber, 54 mg. calcium, 3 mg. iron, 55 mg. vitamin C, 0.9 mg. beta-carotene **Serves 4**

ON THE MENU
Tall, cold drinks are called for here, and cornsticks—cornbread shaped like little ears of corn—would be a fitting bread. For dessert, try an unusual combination: vanilla frozen yogurt topped with just a pinch of freshly ground black pepper.

FOOD FACT
Although beef is the source of much of the fat in the American diet, lean cuts still have a place in low-fat meals. Choose cuts from the round, or rump, such as eye of round, top round, bottom round roast, boneless rump roast and round steak.

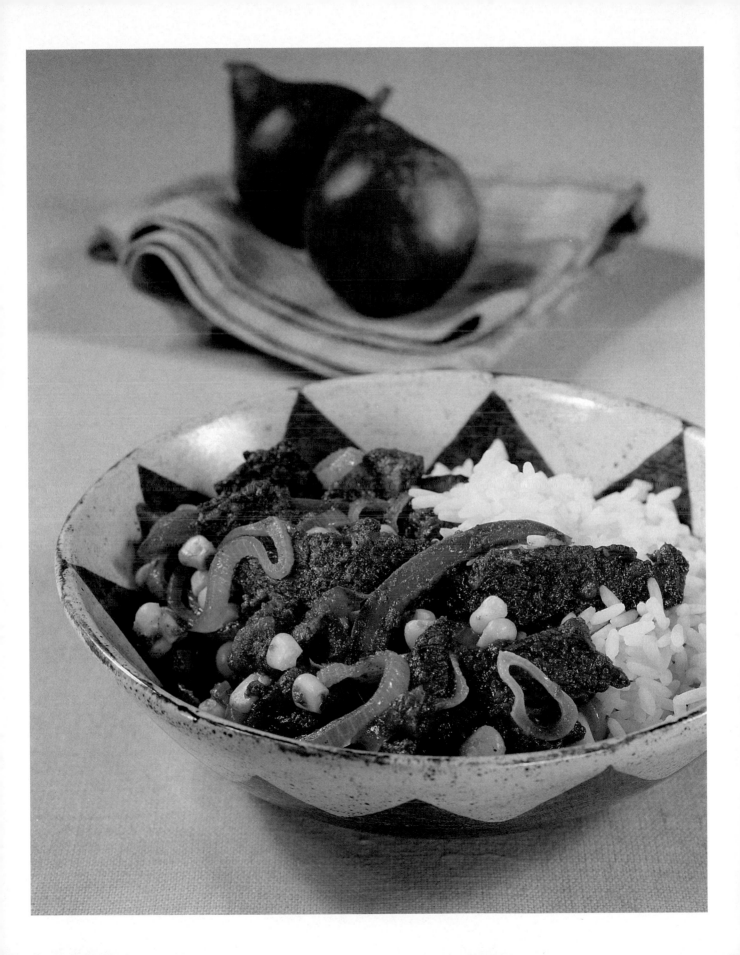

Turkey and Zucchini Parmigiana

1 large Spanish onion, cut into ¼-inch-thick slices

1 tablespoon olive oil

2 garlic cloves, crushed

1 tablespoon water

½ teaspoon dried basil

½ teaspoon dried oregano

¼ teaspoon freshly ground black pepper

¼ teaspoon crushed red pepper flakes

⅛ teaspoon salt

4 thin turkey breast cutlets (12 ounces)

2 medium zucchini, cut into ¼-inch-thick lengthwise slices

1 tablespoon unseasoned dry bread crumbs

1 can (14½ ounces) no-salt-added stewed tomatoes with juice

3 ounces part-skim mozzarella cheese, shredded

1 tablespoon grated Parmesan cheese

Broiling really brings out the flavor of vegetables, especially when they're cooked until lightly charred. The smoky savor of broiled onions and zucchini lends richness to this layering of turkey, vegetables and luscious melted cheese. Serve it with a side dish of your favorite pasta, or with thick slices of Italian peasant bread.

1 Preheat the broiler. Spray a jelly-roll pan with no-stick spray.

2 Arrange the onion slices in a single layer in the prepared pan and drizzle 1 teaspoon of the oil over them. Broil 5 to 6 inches from the heat, turning once, for 10 minutes, or until the onions are tender and lightly charred.

3 Meanwhile, in a cup, mix the remaining 2 teaspoons oil, the garlic, water, basil, oregano, black pepper, red pepper flakes and salt. Brush both sides of the turkey cutlets and zucchini slices with the oil mixture.

4 Using a metal spatula, push the onions toward the center of the pan, arranging them in four stacks. Place the turkey cutlets on top of the onions and arrange the zucchini slices around the edges. Broil for 7 to 9 minutes, or until the turkey is cooked through and the zucchini slices are tender.

5 Preheat the oven to 450°.

6 Sprinkle the bread crumbs in the bottom of a 9 x 9-inch baking dish. Transfer the turkey and onions to the baking dish, then place the zucchini on top.

7 Spoon the tomatoes and their juice over the turkey and vegetables. Sprinkle with the mozzarella and Parmesan, and bake for 10 minutes, or until the sauce is bubbly and the cheeses are melted.

Preparation time 15 minutes • **Total time** 55 minutes • **Per serving** 259 calories, 8.4 g. fat (29% of calories), 3.1 g. saturated fat, 66 mg. cholesterol, 280 mg. sodium, 3.8 g. dietary fiber, 244 mg. calcium, 3 mg. iron, 28 mg. vitamin C, 0.6 mg. beta-carotene • **Serves 4**

Scallop Sauté with Vegetables

¾ **cup raw converted white rice**

1½ **cups water**

1 **pound sea scallops**

1 **tablespoon olive oil**

1 **medium zucchini, halved lengthwise and then cut crosswise into ¼-inch-thick slices**

½ **teaspoon dried basil, crumbled**

⅛ **teaspoon salt**

⅛ **teaspoon freshly ground black pepper**

⅛ **teaspoon crushed red pepper flakes (optional)**

½ **cup diced, drained roasted red peppers (from a jar)**

2 **tablespoons chopped fresh Italian parsley**

S callops, unlike oysters and clams, really have no season: These succulent morsels, enclosed within fanlike shells, are harvested throughout the year on both the East and West coasts. Sweet, tender scallops are almost always sold shucked; the only preparation they sometimes require is the removal of a small piece of tough connective tissue that may remain after shucking.

1 In a heavy, medium saucepan, combine the rice and water; bring to a boil over high heat. Reduce the heat to low, cover and simmer for 20 minutes, or until the rice is tender and the liquid has been absorbed.

2 Meanwhile, rinse and pat dry the scallops. If any of the scallops are very large, cut them in half crosswise.

3 In a large no-stick skillet, warm the oil over high heat. Add the scallops, zucchini, basil, salt, black pepper and red pepper flakes, if using; sauté the scallops and zucchini for 4 to 5 minutes, or until the scallops are opaque at their thickest part and the zucchini slices are tender. Add the roasted red peppers and sauté for 30 seconds longer, or until the peppers are heated through.

4 Remove the skillet from the heat and stir in the parsley. Spoon the scallop mixture over the hot rice.

Preparation time 10 minutes • **Total time** 30 minutes • **Per serving** 271 calories, 4.6 g. fat (15% of calories), 0.6 g. saturated fat, 38 mg. cholesterol, 260 mg. sodium, 0.7 g. dietary fiber, 54 mg. calcium, 3 mg. iron, 27 mg. vitamin C, 0.6 mg. beta-carotene • **Serves 4**

❦ ❦ ❦

If some of the scallops you buy have a rubbery piece of connective tissue on one side, just pull it off with your fingers.

FOR A CHANGE
Use yellow summer squash or pattypan squash instead of zucchini. Subtly flavor the rice with garlic by adding a peeled garlic clove to the cooking water. Remove the garlic before serving.

ON THE MENU
This meal is low enough in calories and fat to be a good choice when you want

to splurge on dessert at a family birthday party or other special occasion. Such an extra-light main dish lets you enjoy a slice of cake with a clear conscience.

FOOD FACT
Red pepper flakes are crushed, dried hot chilies; the seeds are included, making this is a very powerful spice—a pinch or two will usually suffice.

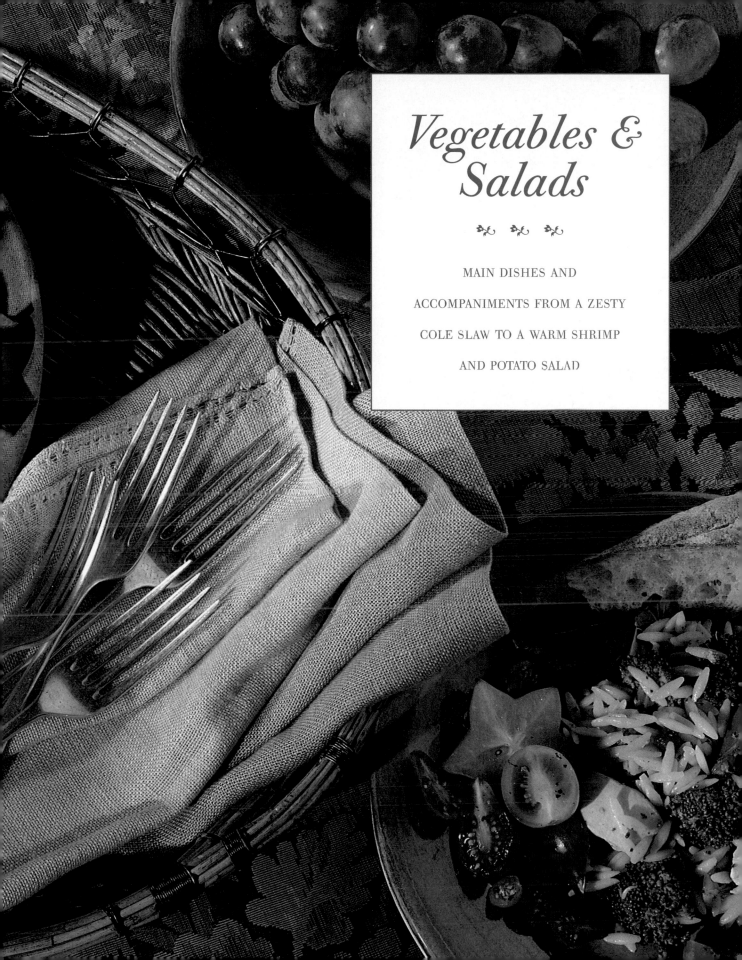

Vegetables & Salads

❧ ❧ ❧

MAIN DISHES AND

ACCOMPANIMENTS FROM A ZESTY

COLE SLAW TO A WARM SHRIMP

AND POTATO SALAD

THREE-BEAN SALAD WITH TURKEY

2 tablespoons unsweetened apple
juice

1 tablespoon plus 2 teaspoons
extra-virgin olive oil

2 tablespoons cider vinegar

1 tablespoon chopped fresh
Italian parsley

1 teaspoon coarse Dijon mustard

½ teaspoon freshly ground black
pepper

¼ teaspoon dried tarragon,
crumbled

1 can (10½ ounces) black beans,
rinsed and drained

1 can (10½ ounces) chick-peas,
rinsed and drained

½ cup chopped red onion

½ cup very thinly sliced celery

12 ounces green beans, trimmed
and cut into ½-inch lengths

6 ounces sliced skinless roast
turkey breast, cut into julienne
strips

Although it's called a vinaigrette, oil—not vinegar—is traditionally the main ingredient in this classic dressing. But you can
tip the proportions in a healthier direction by replacing some
of the oil with broth or, in this case, apple juice. Vary the taste of your
vinaigrette with a selection of vinegars, such as cider, rice-wine and balsamic. The amount of vinegar you use in this recipe depends upon your
personal taste and the sharpness of the vinegar you choose.

1 In a salad bowl, whisk together the apple juice, oil, vinegar, parsley,
mustard, black pepper and tarragon.

2 Add the black beans, chick-peas, onions and celery to the dressing, and toss to coat well. Cover and let stand at room temperature for
10 minutes while you prepare the green beans.

3 In a medium saucepan, bring ½ inch of water to a boil over high
heat. Add the green beans and return to a boil. Reduce the heat to
medium and simmer for 4 to 6 minutes, or until the beans are tender.
Drain in a colander and cool under cold running water.

4 Add the green beans and turkey to the salad bowl, and toss to coat
with the dressing. Taste the salad and add more vinegar if the dressing
seems bland.

Preparation time 15 minutes • **Total time** 40 minutes • **Per serving** 255 calories,
10.2 g. fat (36% of calories), 1.5 g. saturated fat, 36 mg. cholesterol, 290 mg. sodium,
5.6 g. dietary fiber, 71 mg. calcium, 3 mg. iron, 16 mg. vitamin C, 0 mg. beta-carotene
Serves 4

ON THE MENU
Unlike the standard three-bean salad, this
one is a main dish and needs only thick
slices of hearty rye bread or sourdough
peasant bread to make it a meal.

FOR A CHANGE
Use cannellini, kidney or pinto beans
instead of chick-peas. Try yellow wax
beans instead of the green beans, or substitute lean ham for the roast turkey.

*Preceding pages: Warm Chicken and Orzo
Salad (recipe on page 71)*

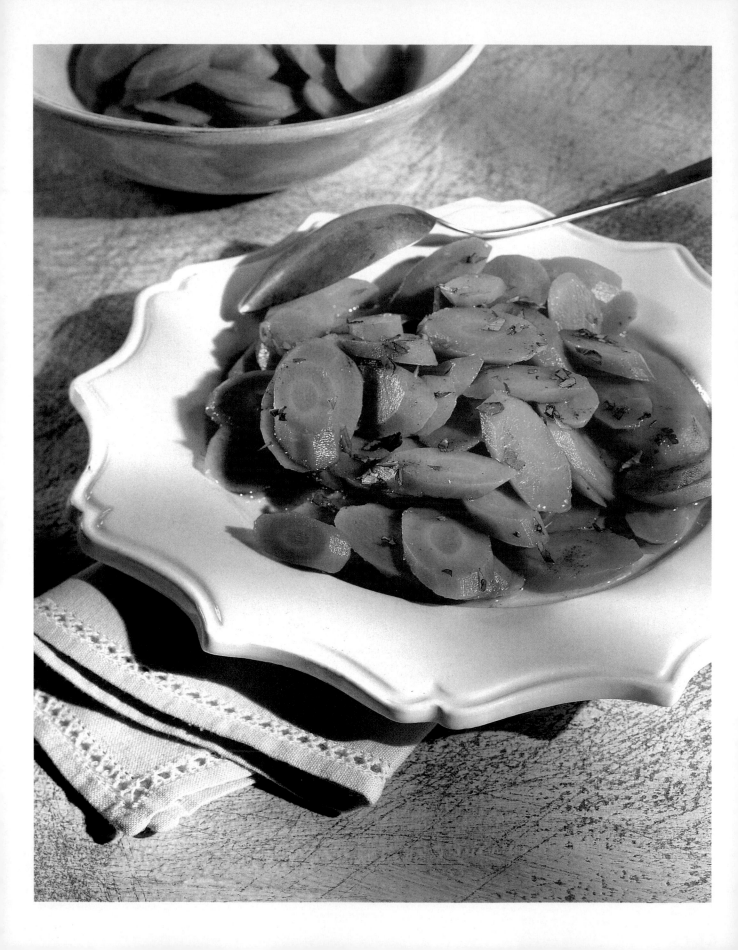

Maple Carrots

8 large carrots, cut into thin diagonal slices

1 tablespoon pure maple syrup

2 teaspoons unsalted butter or margarine

Large pinch of ground cinnamon

Pinch of ground ginger

1 tablespoon chopped fresh cilantro (optional)

Carrots are among the most popular vegetables in America, and it's fortunate that they are so well-liked: A super source of beta-carotene, carrots also provide good amounts of potassium and both soluble and insoluble fiber. Keep carrot sticks on hand for snacks, add grated carrots to salads and sandwiches and, for a change, serve steamed carrot slices, glazed with maple syrup and butter, as an appetizing addition to a simple dinner. Instead of slicing the carrots, you might like to try roll-cutting them (see below).

1 In a deep, medium skillet, bring ½ inch of water to a boil over high heat. Add the carrots and return to a boil. Reduce the heat to medium and simmer for 5 to 6 minutes, or until the carrots are tender. Drain the carrots in a colander; dry the skillet.

2 Add the maple syrup, butter or margarine, cinnamon and ginger to the skillet, and return to medium heat. Cook, stirring constantly, until the butter melts and bubbles. Add the carrots and the cilantro, if using, and toss until the carrots are glazed and heated through.

Preparation time 10 minutes • **Total time** 10 minutes • **Per serving** 66 calories, 2.1 g. fat (28% of calories), 1.2 g. saturated fat, 5 mg. cholesterol, 30 mg. sodium, 2.6 g. dietary fiber, 27 mg. calcium, 1 mg. iron, 8 mg. vitamin C, 14 mg. beta-carotene
Serves 4

❧ ❧ ❧

To roll-cut carrots, first cut off the end of a carrot on a sharp diagonal.

Keeping the knife at the same angle, roll the carrot 180° and make a second cut.

CALICO SLAW WITH POPPYSEED DRESSING

⅓ cup nonfat mayonnaise

1 tablespoon frozen orange juice
concentrate

2 teaspoons fresh lemon juice

1 teaspoon poppy seeds

½ teaspoon honey

¼ teaspoon freshly ground black
pepper

1½ cups finely shredded green
cabbage

1½ cups finely shredded red
cabbage

½ cup thinly sliced red bell
peppers

½ cup stringed and julienne-cut
snow peas

¼ cup coarsely grated carrot

Poppyseed dressing is usually associated with fruit salads, but this citrusy-sweet version is also tasty on a colorful toss of cabbage, peppers, snow peas and carrots. To bring out the flavor of the poppy seeds, cook them in a dry skillet over medium heat just until they smell toasty. Immediately transfer the seeds to a plate and let them cool a bit before adding them to the dressing.

1 In a salad bowl, combine the mayonnaise, orange juice concentrate, lemon juice, poppy seeds, honey and black pepper; whisk together until well blended.

2 Add the green and red cabbages, bell peppers, snow peas and carrots; toss until the vegetables are well coated with the dressing.

Preparation time 25 minutes • **Total time** 25 minutes • **Per serving** 55 calories, 0.5 g. fat (8% of calories), 0 g. saturated fat, 0 mg. cholesterol, 150 mg. sodium, 2.1 g. dietary fiber, 49 mg. calcium, 1 mg. iron, 70 mg. vitamin C, 1.6 mg. beta-carotene • **Serves 4**

❧ ❧ ❧

Cut the head of cabbage in half lengthwise, through its core.

Remove the wedge-shaped core section from each cabbage half.

Halve each half again, then lay each quarter flat on a board and shred it crosswise.

Shrimp and Potato Salad

3 cups water

2 tablespoons plus 2 teaspoons cider vinegar

2 garlic cloves, peeled

1 bay leaf, preferably imported (Turkish)

¼ teaspoon crushed red pepper flakes

⅛ teaspoon salt

12 ounces medium shrimp (thawed if frozen), rinsed

12 ounces small new red potatoes, cut into ½-inch-thick wedges

3 tablespoons reduced-calorie mayonnaise

2 tablespoons plain nonfat yogurt

1 teaspoon Dijon mustard

½ teaspoon celery seed

¼ teaspoon freshly ground black pepper

1 kirby cucumber, thinly sliced

4 radishes, sliced

2 scallions, sliced

The bay leaf may seem an insignificant part of this recipe: After all, it's discarded after cooking, as bay leaves usually are. However, every ingredient counts, and for a more subtle flavor you might try the small Turkish bay leaves rather than the long, narrow domestic ones. Both are available in supermarkets. Like all dried herbs, bay leaves lose their fragrance after a while. If the ones in your spice collection look dusty or browned, it's time to replace them.

1 In a large saucepan, combine the water, 1 tablespoon of the cider vinegar, the garlic, bay leaf, crushed red pepper and salt. Cover and bring to a boil over high heat. Reduce the heat to medium and simmer for 5 minutes to blend the flavors.

2 Add the shrimp to the pot, stir well and simmer for 4 to 5 minutes, or until the shrimp turn pink and firm. Using a slotted spoon (reserve the cooking liquid), transfer the shrimp to a bowl. Rinse briefly with cold water until cool enough to handle and set aside.

3 Add the potatoes to the pot of cooking liquid; increase the heat to high, cover and bring to a boil. Meanwhile, peel and devein the shrimp.

4 Reduce the heat to medium-low and simmer the potatoes for 10 to 15 minutes, or until fork-tender. Reserving 1 tablespoon of the cooking liquid for the dressing, drain the potatoes in a colander; remove and discard the garlic cloves and bay leaf. Transfer the potatoes to a salad bowl and set aside.

5 In a cup, mix the reserved cooking liquid with the remaining 1 tablespoon plus 2 teaspoons cider vinegar, the mayonnaise, yogurt, mustard, celery seeds and black pepper.

6 Add the shrimp, cucumbers, radishes and scallions to the potatoes, then pour on the dressing and toss to coat well.

Preparation time 15 minutes • **Total time** 45 minutes • **Per serving** 187 calories, 4.6 g. fat (22% of calories), 1 g. saturated fat, 109 mg. cholesterol, 248 mg. sodium, 1.9 g. dietary fiber, 67 mg. calcium, 3 mg. iron, 17 mg. vitamin C, 0 mg. beta-carotene
Serves 4

WARM CHICKEN AND ORZO SALAD

- 6 ounces orzo or other small pasta
- 1¾ cups defatted reduced-sodium chicken broth
- ½ cup water
- 12 ounces boneless, skinless chicken breasts, trimmed and cut into 1-inch chunks
- 4 cups broccoli florets
- ¼ cup packed Italian parsley sprigs
- 2 tablespoons extra-virgin olive oil
- 2 tablespoons red wine vinegar
- 1 tablespoon Dijon mustard
- ¼ teaspoon salt
- ½ teaspoon freshly ground black pepper
- 1 garlic clove, peeled
- ¼ cup diced, drained roasted red peppers (from a jar)

Pasta salads, often party fare, also make delightful family dinners. This one starts with the tried-and-true pairing of chicken and rice, but the "rice" is really orzo, a grain-shaped pasta. The dish tastes best when served warm, but if necessary, you can prepare it ahead of time and refrigerate it. Just be sure to take the salad out of the refrigerator a little while before serving time so that it can return to room temperature.

1 Bring a covered medium saucepan of water to a boil over high heat. Add the pasta to the boiling water, return to a boil and cook for 8 to 10 minutes or according to package directions until al dente. Drain in a colander, rinse briefly under cold running water and drain again. Transfer the pasta to a large salad bowl.

2 While the pasta is cooking, bring 1½ cups of the broth and the water to a boil in a medium skillet. Add the chicken and return to a boil. Reduce the heat to medium-low, cover and simmer, stirring occasionally, for 6 to 8 minutes, or until the chicken is cooked through. Using a slotted spoon, transfer the chicken to the bowl of orzo; reserve the broth in the skillet.

3 Return the broth to a boil over high heat. Add the broccoli and return to a boil. Cook for 3 to 5 minutes, or until the broccoli is crisp-tender. Drain the broccoli in a colander, cool briefly under cold running water and drain again. Add the broccoli to the bowl of orzo.

4 Combine the parsley, oil, vinegar, mustard, salt, black pepper and the remaining ¼ cup broth in a food processor. With the processor running, drop the garlic clove through the feed tube; process the mixture until puréed.

5 Pour the dressing over the pasta mixture. Add the roasted peppers and toss the salad to mix well. Serve warm.

Preparation time 10 minutes • **Total time** 20 minutes • **Per serving** 365 calories, 9.4 g. fat (23% of calories), 1.4 g. saturated fat, 49 mg. cholesterol, 400 mg. sodium, 5.8 g. dietary fiber, 83 mg. calcium, 4 mg. iron, 109 mg. vitamin C, 2 mg. beta-carotene • **Serves 4**

BUTTERMILK MASHED POTATOES

1 pound baking potatoes, such as russets, peeled and cut into 1-inch chunks

1 cup water

½ cup defatted chicken broth

2 garlic cloves, unpeeled

¼ cup low-fat buttermilk

2 tablespoons thinly sliced scallions

⅛ teaspoon freshly ground pepper, preferably white

Large pinch of salt

Mashed potatoes give meals the comforting taste of home. Traditionally, the potatoes would be finished with butter and cream, but there are other ways to add richness: For this recipe, the potatoes are cooked in broth with garlic cloves, then mashed with buttermilk and sliced scallions. Mash the potatoes smooth, or leave them truly "homestyle"—a bit lumpy.

1 In a medium saucepan, combine the potatoes, water, broth and garlic cloves. Cover and bring to a boil over high heat. Reduce the heat to medium-low and simmer for 12 to 15 minutes, or until the potatoes are fork-tender.

2 Just before the potatoes are done, place the buttermilk in a small, heavy saucepan and warm it over low heat.

3 Drain the potatoes well; discard the garlic cloves. Return the potatoes to the pan and mash them with a potato masher.

4 Stir the warmed buttermilk, scallions, ground pepper and salt into the potatoes and serve.

Preparation time 10 minutes • **Total time** 30 minutes • **Per serving** 96 calories, 0.5 g. fat (5% of calories), 0.1 g. saturated fat, 1 mg. cholesterol, 191 mg. sodium, 1.8 g. dietary fiber, 24 mg. calcium, 1 mg. iron, 17 mg. vitamin C, 0 mg. beta-carotene
Serves 4

This type of potato masher requires a fair amount of pressure.

The more open wire masher is a little easier to use because there's less resistance.

An electric mixer on low speed is the easiest way to mash potatoes.

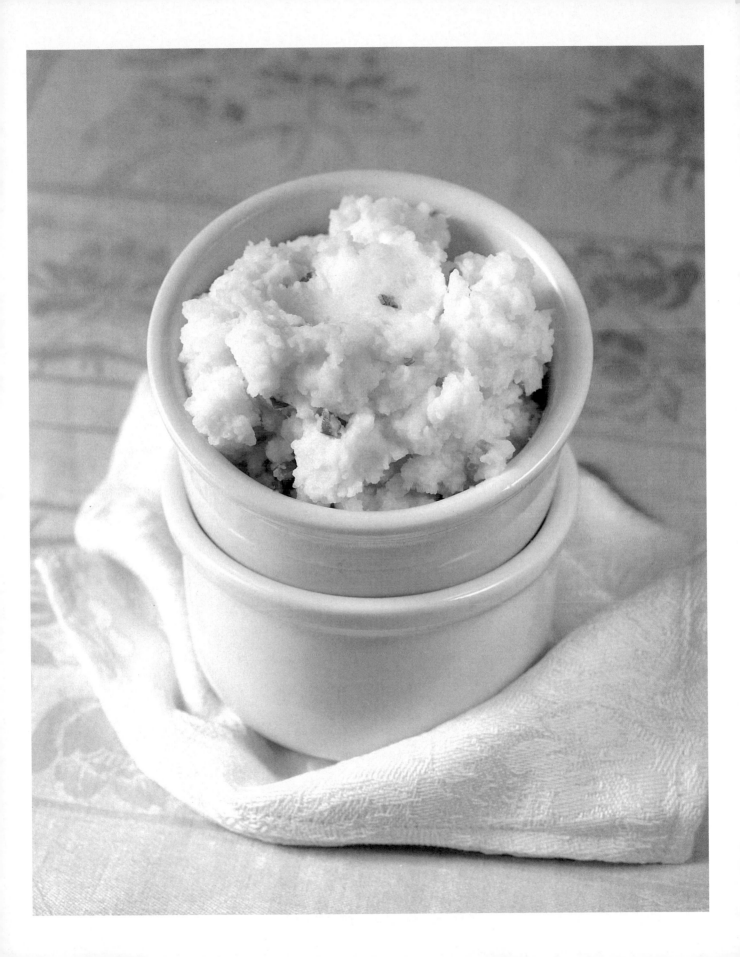

BROCCOLI WITH CORN AND CRISP GARLIC

1 lemon

3 cups small broccoli florets

¾ cup frozen corn kernels

1 teaspoon extra-virgin olive oil

3 garlic cloves, thinly sliced

¼ teaspoon freshly ground black
pepper

⅛ teaspoon salt

As readily available as broccoli is today, it wasn't until the mid-20th century that this vegetable gained popularity in the United States. In Italy, where broccoli has been a mainstay for centuries, it is often dressed, as it is here, with garlicky oil.

1 Using a swivel-bladed vegetable peeler, remove 2 or 3 wide bands of zest from the lemon; cut enough zest into thin strips to measure a scant tablespoon. Squeeze 1 tablespoon of juice from the lemon.

2 In a covered, deep medium skillet, bring ½ inch of water to a boil over high heat. Add the broccoli and return to a boil. Cook, turning the pieces occasionally, for 3 to 4 minutes, or until the broccoli is crisp-tender. Add the corn during the last minute or so of cooking time. Drain the broccoli and corn in a colander, and transfer to a heated platter; cover and keep warm.

3 In a small skillet, warm the oil over medium heat. Add the garlic, black pepper and salt, and sauté, stirring constantly, for about 1 minute, or until the garlic just begins to brown. Add the lemon zest and lemon juice, and stir to combine; immediately pour the garlic mixture over the broccoli and corn.

Preparation time 10 minutes • **Total time** 25 minutes • **Per serving** 72 calories, 1.7 g. fat (21% of calories), 0.2 g. saturated fat, 0 mg. cholesterol, 94 mg. sodium, 4 g. dietary fiber, 49 mg. calcium, 1 mg. iron, 0 mg. vitamin C, 1 mg. beta-carotene
Serves 4

First, shave wide strips of peel from the lemon, removing only the colored zest.

Then, with a sharp paring knife, cut each piece of lemon zest into thin strips.

MASHED SWEET POTATOES WITH HONEY

1 pound sweet potatoes, peeled
   and cut into 1-inch chunks

¼ cup apricot nectar

1 tablespoon honey

⅛ teaspoon ground cinnamon

Large pinch of freshly ground
black pepper

It seems a pity to serve sweet potatoes only during the holidays—and it's practically a crime to bury their velvety texture and wonderful natural sweetness under a layer of marshmallows and brown sugar. This notably nutritious vegetable, available all year round in most supermarkets, can be boiled, steamed, baked, roasted or even grilled. Bring out the sweet potato's savory side with the same toppings you'd use for white potatoes—such as yogurt and chives—or enhance its sweetness with a touch of honey and some apricot nectar.

1 Place the sweet potatoes in a medium saucepan and add enough cold water to cover them. Cover the pan and bring to a boil over high heat. Reduce the heat to medium-low and simmer for 12 to 15 minutes, or until the potatoes are fork-tender.

2 Meanwhile, in a small saucepan, warm the apricot nectar over medium-low heat.

3 Drain the potatoes in a colander and return them to the saucepan in which they were cooked. Add the apricot nectar, honey, cinnamon and black pepper, and mash until smooth.

Preparation time 10 minutes • **Total time** 35 minutes • **Per serving** 111 calories, 0.3 g. fat (2% of calories), 0 g. saturated fat, 0 mg. cholesterol, 11 mg. sodium, 0.5 g. dietary fiber, 20 mg. calcium, 1 mg. iron, 27 mg. vitamin C, 10 mg. beta-carotene • **Serves 4**

MARKET AND PANTRY
Although sweet potatoes look quite sturdy, they are highly susceptible to decay. Buy potatoes that are smooth, firm and free of shriveled or dark areas. Store them in a cool, dry place (about 55° is best), not in the refrigerator, where their natural sugars will turn to starch, robbing the potatoes of their unique flavor.

FOR A CHANGE
Season the mashed sweet potatoes with nutmeg, allspice, ginger or cloves.

ON THE MENU
These lightly sweet and spicy potatoes are delicious with pork or poultry. For a holiday meal, offer both mashed sweet and white potatoes.

ROMAINE SALAD WITH PEPPER DRESSING

3 tablespoons nonfat sour cream

2 tablespoons low-fat buttermilk

2 teaspoons red wine vinegar

½ teaspoon coarsely ground black pepper

⅛ teaspoon celery seeds

⅛ teaspoon salt

3 cups cut-up romaine lettuce (1-inch pieces)

¾ cup sliced radishes

Although green salads are virtually fat-free, commercial salad dressings can turn a plate of lettuce into the fattiest part of the meal. Two tablespoons of blue-cheese dressing, for instance—the amount a salad-bar ladle might hold—can add 14 grams of fat. The packet of dressing that accompanies a fast-food salad may contain as much as 30 grams of fat. Of course, this doesn't mean you have to settle for a "naked" salad: Just base your dressing on low-fat ingredients, such as the buttermilk and nonfat sour cream used here. For a change, make the salad with red-leaf lettuce or radicchio and use white radishes (see below).

1 In a salad bowl, combine the sour cream, buttermilk, vinegar, black pepper, celery seeds and salt; whisk with a fork until blended.

2 Add the romaine and the radishes, and toss to coat well with the dressing.

Preparation time 15 minutes • **Total time** 15 minutes • **Per serving** 22 calories, 0.3 g. fat (10% of calories), 0 g. saturated fat, 0 mg. cholesterol, 94 mg. sodium, 1.2 g. dietary fiber, 46 mg. calcium, 1 mg. iron, 15 mg. vitamin C, 0.7 mg. beta-carotene • **Serves 4**

❧   ❧   ❧

Red "button" radishes, the most familiar type, are available everywhere.

Mild-tasting white icicle radishes, like button radishes, do not require peeling.

Sharp-flavored daikon, a giant Japanese radish, should be peeled before using.

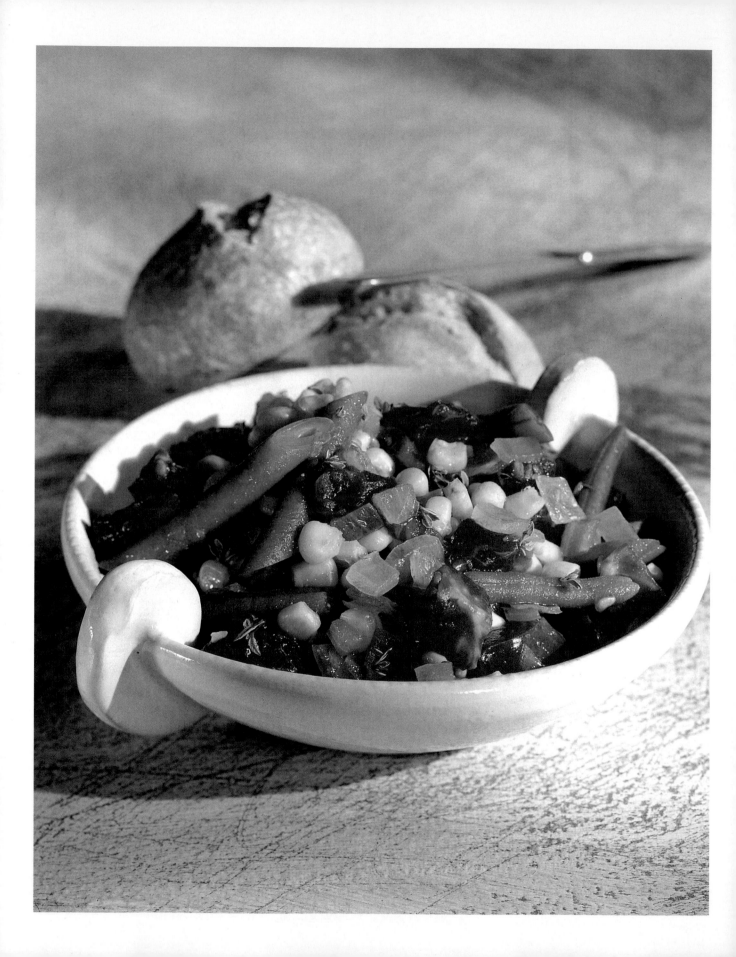

Tomato and Corn Succotash

1 cup trimmed, halved green beans

1 teaspoon olive oil

1 medium onion, chopped

1 garlic clove, minced

¼ teaspoon dried thyme, crumbled

⅛ teaspoon freshly ground black pepper

⅛ teaspoon salt

Large pinch of sugar

2 tablespoons defatted chicken broth or water

2 small ripe tomatoes, coarsely chopped

1 cup fresh or frozen corn kernels

As prepared in colonial America, succotash was a simple stew of corn and lima beans, enriched with salt pork and milk. The dish evolved in time, with the addition of other seasonal ingredients—such as bell peppers and tomatoes—and creative seasonings. For this colorful rendition, fresh corn is combined with green beans and tomatoes; the flavor is accentuated with onions, garlic and thyme.

1 In a deep medium skillet, bring ½ inch of water to a boil over high heat. Add the green beans and return to a boil. Cook for 3 to 5 minutes, stirring occasionally, until the beans are crisp-tender. Drain the beans in a colander; dry the skillet.

2 Add the oil to the same skillet, then stir in the onions, garlic, thyme, black pepper, salt and sugar. Sauté over medium-high heat for 1 minute, then stir in 1 tablespoon of the broth or water and sauté for 4 to 5 minutes, or until the onions are tender.

3 Stir in the blanched green beans, the tomatoes, corn and the remaining 1 tablespoon broth or water, and bring to a simmer. Reduce the heat to medium-low, cover and simmer, stirring occasionally, for 5 minutes, or until the tomatoes release their juices and all the vegetables are tender.

Preparation time 10 minutes • **Total time** 35 minutes • **Per serving** 81 calories, 1.9 g. fat (21% of calories), 0.2 g. saturated fat, 0 mg. cholesterol, 114 mg. sodium, 3.1 g. dietary fiber, 26 mg. calcium, 1 mg. iron, 20 mg. vitamin C, 0.4 mg. beta-carotene • **Serves 4**

MARKET AND PANTRY
Corn loses its natural sweetness very quickly after it's picked. Short of growing your own corn, the best guarantee of freshness is to buy corn at the farm where it is harvested, or at a farmer's market.

KITCHEN TIP
You can buy a special cutter to remove the kernels from fresh corn: This metal trough, about the size of an ear of corn, has a center opening fitted with blades. When you slide an ear of corn across the blades, they cut off the kernels, which drop through the opening. It's easy to cut the kernels from corn with a knife, too. Trim one end of an ear of corn so that you can stand it upright on a cutting board. Slide the blade of a sharp knife down the ear to cut off the kernels. Press gently so that you don't cut off any of the fibrous cob along with the tender kernels.

SPINACH WITH MUSHROOMS

2 large shallots or 1 small onion, chopped

¼ cup defatted chicken broth or water

¾ teaspoon olive oil

4 ounces small fresh mushrooms, quartered

1 pound washed spinach, tough stems removed

⅛ teaspoon salt

⅛ teaspoon freshly ground black pepper

We've come a long way since the time when cookbooks directed that spinach and other tender greens be "stewed" for half an hour, turning them into a gray mush with little nutritional value. When spinach is cooked just long enough to wilt it, the leaves stay a vibrant green and little of the vitamin C is lost.

1 In a large no-stick skillet, combine the shallots or onions, 2 tablespoons of the broth or water and the oil. Place the skillet over medium-high heat and cook, stirring constantly, for 3 to 4 minutes, or until the shallots or onions are tender.

2 Add the mushrooms and the remaining 2 tablespoons broth or water, and cook, stirring frequently, for 4 to 6 minutes, or until the mushrooms are tender.

3 Increase the heat to high. Add the spinach by handfuls and stir constantly until the spinach wilts; cook for 1 minute longer, season with the salt and pepper, and serve.

Preparation time 15 minutes • **Total time** 25 minutes • **Per serving** 39 calories, 1.3 g. fat (30% of calories), 0.2 g. saturated fat, 0 mg. cholesterol, 197 mg. sodium, 2.5 g. dietary fiber, 86 mg. calcium, 3 mg. iron, 24 mg. vitamin C, 3 mg. beta-carotene
Serves 4

Wash the spinach and gently pat it dry with a kitchen towel.

Hold the leaves between your fingers and pull off the stem from each leaf.

MEXICAN TACO SALAD

4 corn tortillas

8 ounces lean, trimmed beef top round

1 tablespoon chili powder

½ teaspoon olive oil

2 tablespoons defatted beef broth

1 large tomato, diced

1 can (10½ ounces) pinto beans or red kidney beans, rinsed and drained

1 tablespoon chopped, seeded canned jalapeño chilies (optional)

2 cups shredded iceberg lettuce

1 small red onion, sliced

1 tablespoon fresh lime juice

1½ ounces Cheddar cheese, shredded

¼ cup chopped fresh cilantro

You're far better off making a taco salad at home than ordering one at a fast-food restaurant. Served with a deep-fried flour tortilla, cheese, sour cream and dressing, one popular fast-food taco salad packs about 900 calories and 60 grams of fat—a terrific incentive to shop for some lean, flavorful ingredients and assemble this beefy salad in your own kitchen.

1 Preheat the oven to 400°.

2 Stack the tortillas and cut them into 8 wedges each. Arrange the tortilla wedges in a single layer on a baking sheet and bake for 8 to 10 minutes, or until crisp and lightly browned. Remove the baking sheet from the oven and let the tortilla chips cool on the baking sheet.

3 While the tortilla chips are baking, cut the beef into cubes and process in a food processor until finely ground. Add the chili powder and pulse just until mixed.

4 In a medium no-stick skillet, warm the oil over high heat until hot but not smoking. Crumble in the beef, add the broth and sauté for 2 to 3 minutes, or until the meat is no longer pink. Add the tomatoes, beans and jalapeños, if using, and sauté for 3 to 4 minutes, or until the tomatoes are softened and the mixture is just heated through.

5 Arrange the shredded lettuce and onions in a shallow serving bowl; drizzle with the lime juice. Spoon the beef mixture on top and sprinkle the Cheddar over it. Scatter the tortilla chips around the beef and sprinkle with the cilantro.

Preparation time 15 minutes • **Total time** 35 minutes • **Per serving** 249 calories, 7.5 g. fat (27% of calories), 3.1 g. saturated fat, 44 mg. cholesterol, 310 mg. sodium, 5.2 g. dietary fiber, 172 mg. calcium, 3 mg. iron, 18 mg. vitamin C, 1 mg. beta-carotene • **Serves 4**

Stack the tortillas and cut them in half, then stack the two halves and cut them into wedges.

ON THE MENU

Accompany the taco salad with your favorite bottled salsa. Offer a refreshing pitcher of pink lemonade, made by mixing a small amount of cranberry juice into fresh lemonade. For a dessert with Mexican flair, dust scoops of chocolate frozen yogurt with ground cinnamon.

Pastas & Grains

❧ ❧ ❧

A BARLEY BAKE, MACARONI AND
CHEESE, SPAGHETTI WITH RED SAUCE
AND RICE WITH A TWIST: SUSTAINING
STARCHES THAT MAKE THE MEAL

SPAGHETTI WITH HEARTY RED SAUCE

6 ounces skinless turkey breast, cut into 1-inch chunks

1 medium onion, cut into quarters

3 garlic cloves, peeled

½ teaspoon dried oregano, crumbled

½ teaspoon dried basil, crumbled

½ teaspoon freshly ground black pepper

2 teaspoons olive oil

1 can (16 ounces) crushed tomatoes

2 tablespoons no-salt-added tomato paste

2 tablespoons dry red wine or defatted beef broth

⅛ teaspoon salt

8 ounces spaghetti

2 tablespoons chopped fresh Italian parsley

1 tablespoon grated Parmesan cheese

Many pasta lovers believe that a great tomato sauce must be simmered for hours, painstakingly stirred, seasoned and tasted by an old-world cook. This picturesque image is not very appealing, however, to someone with limited kitchen time. Rather than opening a jar, spend a worthwhile half hour on a family-pleasing sauce that's homemade right down to the freshly ground turkey.

1 Bring a large covered pot of water to a boil over high heat.

2 Meanwhile, process the turkey in a food processor until finely chopped; transfer the turkey to a bowl. In the food processor, finely chop the onions and garlic. Return the ground turkey to the processor, add the oregano, basil and black pepper, and pulse just until mixed.

3 In a large, heavy saucepan, warm the oil over high heat until very hot but not smoking. Crumble in the turkey mixture and cook, stirring often, for 4 to 6 minutes, or until the turkey turns white. Stir in the tomatoes, tomato paste, wine or broth and salt, and bring to a boil. Reduce the heat to low, cover and simmer, stirring occasionally, for 15 minutes.

4 While the sauce is cooking, add the pasta to the boiling water, return to a boil and cook for 10 minutes or according to package directions until al dente. Drain in a colander and transfer to a warmed serving bowl.

5 Stir the parsley into the sauce. Pour the sauce over the pasta and sprinkle with the Parmesan.

Preparation time 15 minutes • **Total time** 30 minutes • **Per serving** 340 calories, 4.2 g. fat (11% of calories), 0.8 g. saturated fat, 27 mg. cholesterol, 310 mg. sodium, 3.4 g. dietary fiber, 88 mg. calcium, 4 mg. iron, 26 mg. vitamin C, 0.6 mg. beta-carotene • **Serves 4**

FOR A CHANGE
Americans seem to have settled on spaghetti as the "right" pasta for this type of sauce, but it's also good with sturdy pastas such as rigatoni or ziti, or any of the thick pasta strands, such as fettuccine, tagliatelle or perciatelli, which is a hollow version of spaghetti.

Preceding pages: Penne with Chicken Marengo (recipe on page 103)

SESAME AND LEEK RICE PILAF

1½ teaspoons sesame seeds

1¼ cups water

½ cup defatted reduced-sodium chicken broth

1 teaspoon dark sesame oil

½ cup thinly sliced leeks (white and green part)

¾ cup raw converted white rice

¼ teaspoon freshly ground black pepper

⅛ teaspoon salt

Pilafs made from rice or other grains are centuries-old mainstays throughout the Near East, India and some parts of Europe. Spanish paella, for instance—a lavish dish of saffron-tinted rice, meat, shellfish and vegetables—is a form of pilaf. The common denominator is that the grain must be sautéed before being cooked in broth.

1 Place the sesame seeds in a small skillet and toast over medium-high heat, tossing frequently, for 3 to 4 minutes, or until lightly browned. Immediately transfer the sesame seeds to a small plate.

2 In a small saucepan, bring the water and broth to a boil over high heat. Remove the pan from the heat.

3 In a heavy, medium saucepan, warm the oil over medium heat until very hot but not smoking. Stir in the leeks and sauté for 3 to 4 minutes, or until just tender. Add the rice and sesame seeds, and stir to mix with the leeks.

4 Pour the hot broth mixture into the pan of rice, then stir in the black pepper and salt.

5 Increase the heat to high and bring to a boil. Reduce the heat to low, cover and cook for 20 to 25 minutes, or until the rice is tender and the liquid has been absorbed.

As soon as the sesame seeds begin to color and become fragrant, tip them onto a plate; they will overcook if left in the hot skillet.

Preparation time 10 minutes • **Total time** 45 minutes • **Per serving** 156 calories, 2 g. fat (12% of calories), 0.3 g. saturated fat, 0 mg. cholesterol, 154 mg. sodium, 0.8 g. dietary fiber, 41 mg. calcium, 2 mg. iron, 2 mg. vitamin C, 0 mg. beta-carotene
Serves 4

MARKET AND PANTRY
Oriental sesame oil may not have been in your mother's pantry, but it's become a staple for many of today's cooks. Unlike neutral vegetable oils (such as corn or soybean), dark sesame oil has a singularly rich flavor and nutlike fragrance. It is more often used for flavoring than as a cooking oil, but in this recipe it serves both purposes.

ON THE MENU
Serve the pilaf with grilled chicken, peppers and mushrooms. Finish the meal with skewered tropical fruits, brushed with lime juice and honey and grilled.

BACON AND ONION MACARONI

- 1 tablespoon plus 1 teaspoon olive oil
- 2 large onions, sliced
- 4 garlic cloves, minced
- ½ teaspoon dried basil, crumbled
- 8 ounces macaroni, such as ribbed elbows
- 2 cans (8 ounces each) no-salt-added tomatoes with juice
- 3 ounces trimmed Canadian bacon or lean ham, cut into ¼-inch pieces
- ¼ cup drained, seeded, sliced peperoncini or drained, canned chopped green chilies
- ⅛ teaspoon crushed red pepper flakes
- 2 tablespoons no-salt-added tomato paste

You can easily remove the seeds from the peperoncini with the tip of a teaspoon.

Even bacon can have a place in a healthful diet, if it is eaten in moderation. Canadian bacon has about one-fifth the fat (and less than half the calories) of regular bacon, and just three ounces of bacon flavor four servings of this simple, hearty dish. A virtually fat-free ingredient that you can use with abandon is Italian peperoncini. These slender pickled peppers are slightly hot, so canned green chilies make a good substitute for the Italian version.

1 Bring a large covered pot of water to a boil over high heat.

2 In a large, heavy no-stick skillet, warm the oil over high heat until very hot but not smoking. Add the onions, garlic and basil, and stir to coat well with the oil. When the onions begin to soften, reduce the heat to medium. Cover and cook, stirring frequently, for 10 minutes, or until the onions are very tender. (Reduce the heat if the onions seem to be sticking to the pan.)

3 Add the pasta to the boiling water, return to a boil and cook for 8 to 10 minutes or according to package directions until al dente. Drain in a colander.

4 While the pasta is cooking, drain and reserve the juice from the tomatoes. Coarsely chop the tomatoes; set aside.

5 Add the bacon or ham, peperoncini or chilies and crushed red pepper flakes to the skillet; increase the heat to medium-high and sauté for 2 to 3 minutes, or until heated through.

6 Stir in the chopped tomatoes with their juice and the tomato paste; bring to a boil. Reduce the heat to medium, cover and simmer, stirring occasionally, for 5 minutes, or until the flavors are blended.

7 Add the drained macaroni to the sauce; toss until well mixed and heated through.

Preparation time 12 minutes • **Total time** 30 minutes • **Per serving** 363 calories, 7.4 g. fat (18% of calories), 1.3 g. saturated fat, 11 mg. cholesterol, 380 mg. sodium, 4.5 g. dietary fiber, 77 mg. calcium, 4 mg. iron, 39 mg. vitamin C, 0.6 mg. beta-carotene • **Serves 4**

Fusilli with Three-Greens Pesto

3 cups loosely packed fresh spinach, washed and trimmed

½ cup loosely packed Italian parsley sprigs

3 scallions, cut into 1-inch pieces

1 ounce Parmesan cheese, grated

¼ cup defatted reduced-sodium chicken broth, vegetable broth or water

1 tablespoon extra-virgin olive oil

1 tablespoon fresh lemon juice

½ teaspoon freshly ground black pepper

¼ teaspoon salt

2 garlic cloves, peeled

8 ounces long fusilli

2 cups thinly sliced carrots

Instead of the more usual basil, this pesto is made with spinach, parsley and scallions, their refreshingly "green" flavors sparked with garlic and Parmesan. Unlike more liquid sauces, thick pesto—literally "paste"—often needs to be thinned a bit: Just save a few spoonfuls of the cooking water for this purpose when you drain the pasta and stir the hot water into the pesto.

1 Bring a large covered pot of water to a boil over high heat.

2 Meanwhile, place the spinach, parsley, scallions, 2 tablespoons of the Parmesan, the broth or water, oil, lemon juice, black pepper and salt in a food processor. With the processor running, drop the garlic cloves through the feed tube and process until puréed.

3 Add the pasta to the boiling water, return to a boil and cook for 5 minutes, then add the carrots and cook for 5 to 7 minutes longer, or until the pasta is al dente. Reserving about 2 tablespoons of the cooking water, drain the pasta and carrots in a colander.

4 Transfer the pasta and carrots to a warmed serving bowl. Add the pesto and the reserved cooking water, and toss to mix well. Sprinkle with the remaining 2 tablespoons Parmesan and serve.

Preparation time 10 minutes • **Total time** 25 minutes • **Per serving** 310 calories, 6.3 g. fat (18% of calories), 1.6 g. saturated fat, 4 mg. cholesterol, 339 mg. sodium, 5.2 g. dietary fiber, 171 mg. calcium, 5 mg. iron, 33 mg. vitamin C, 12 mg. beta-carotene • **Serves 4**

Italian parsley, also called flat-leaf parsley, is more strongly flavored than the curly type. Use only crisp, green sprigs, discarding any wilted or yellow leaves.

HEAD START
The pesto can be made a few hours ahead of time and refrigerated until it is needed. Place the pesto in a small container, place a piece of plastic wrap on the surface (otherwise the mixture may darken), then cover the container. You can also slice the carrots ahead of time; toss them with a few drops of lemon juice to preserve their color.

KITCHEN TIPS
Cooking the carrots with the pasta saves you washing an extra pot. Slice the carrots very thinly so they cook quickly; drain the pasta as soon as it is al dente, rather than waiting for the carrots to become tender.

FOR A CHANGE
Serve Three-Greens Pesto over filled pasta such as cheese tortellini or ravioli.

Pasta with Turkey and Fresh Salsa

2 large ripe tomatoes, cut into chunks

1 medium green bell pepper, cut into chunks

½ cup coarsely chopped Spanish onion or red onion

½ cup cilantro sprigs

2 tablespoons fresh lime juice

1 tablespoon extra-virgin olive oil

½ teaspoon salt

½ teaspoon freshly ground black pepper

⅛–¼ teaspoon hot-pepper sauce or to taste

8 ounces thin-sliced turkey-breast cutlets, cut into ½ x 2-inch strips

1½ teaspoons ground cumin

8 ounces wagon-wheel pasta

The lively condiment we know as salsa is what Mexican cooks call *salsa cruda,* literally "raw sauce." The most familiar salsa cruda is a mixture of chopped fresh tomatoes, onions, chilies, lime juice and cilantro. Homemade salsa is a delightful change from cooked pasta sauces: Teamed with fun-to-eat wagon-wheel pasta and broiled turkey strips, it makes a tasty and substantial meal.

1 Bring a large covered pot of water to a boil over high heat.

2 Meanwhile, combine the tomatoes, bell peppers, onions and cilantro in a food processor and pulse just until finely chopped. Transfer to a large serving bowl. Stir in 1 tablespoon of the lime juice, the oil, ¼ teaspoon each of the salt and black pepper, and the hot-pepper sauce; set the salsa aside.

3 In a shallow bowl, toss the turkey strips with the remaining 1 tablespoon lime juice, the remaining ¼ teaspoon each salt and black pepper and the cumin; set aside.

4 Add the pasta to the boiling water, return to a boil and cook for 7 to 9 minutes or according to package directions until al dente; drain in a colander.

5 While the pasta is cooking, preheat the broiler. Spray a jelly-roll pan with no-stick spray.

6 Arrange the turkey in a single layer on the prepared jelly-roll pan; broil 3 to 4 inches from the heat for 3 to 4 minutes, or until cooked through.

7 Add the pasta to the bowl of salsa, then add the turkey and any cooking juices from the pan; toss to coat the pasta and turkey with the sauce.

Preparation time 20 minutes • **Total time** 35 minutes • **Per serving** 338 calories, 5.2 g. fat (14% of calories), 0.8 g. saturated fat, 35 mg. cholesterol, 323 mg. sodium, 3 g. dietary fiber, 40 mg. calcium, 4 mg. iron, 36 mg. vitamin C, 0.4 mg. beta-carotene
Serves 4

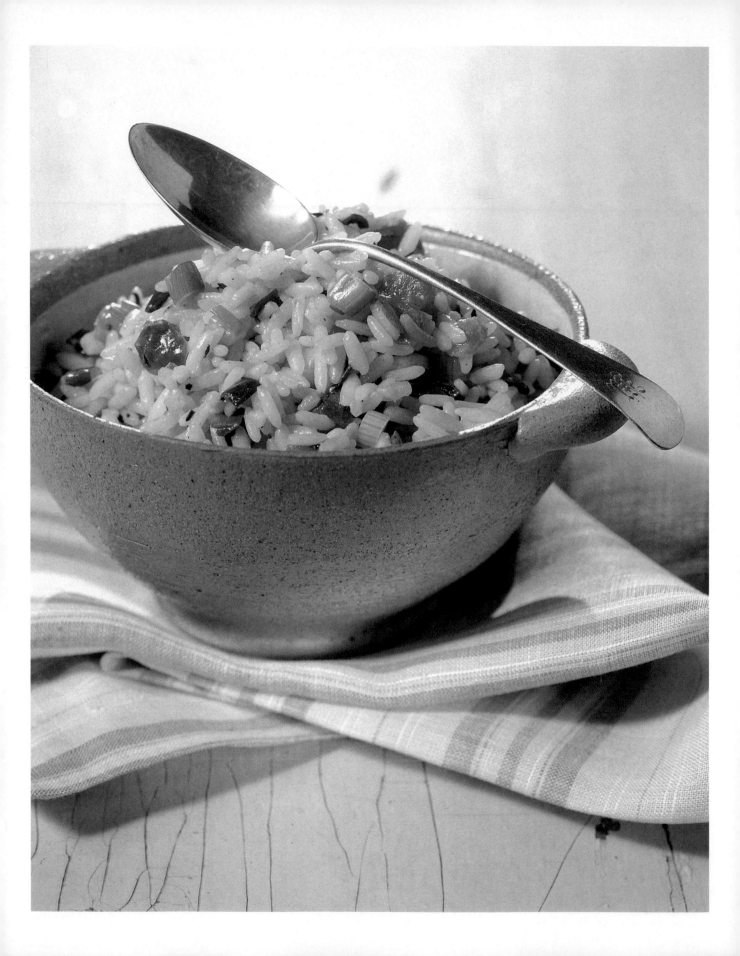

TOMATO AND MOZZARELLA RICE

½ **cup plus 2 tablespoons defatted reduced-sodium chicken broth**

1 **large ripe plum tomato, diced**

3 **scallions, sliced**

1 **garlic clove, minced**

⅛ **teaspoon salt**

½ **cup raw converted white rice**

½ **cup water**

¼ **teaspoon freshly ground black pepper**

¼ **teaspoon dried thyme, crumbled**

¼ **teaspoon dried basil, crumbled**

1 **tablespoon plus 2 teaspoons part-skim mozzarella, shredded**

A slice of pizza does not spring to mind as the ideal side dish for a healthful dinner, but this zesty rice may remind you of your favorite cheese-topped slice. It contains many of the same ingredients—tomatoes, mozzarella, garlic and herbs—but the fat content is minimal. Spoon the rice alongside turkey burgers or baked chicken breasts and even "junk food junkies" will clean their plates.

1 In a heavy, medium saucepan, combine 2 tablespoons of the broth, the diced tomatoes, scallions, garlic and salt; sauté over high heat for 3 to 4 minutes, or until the scallions are wilted, the tomatoes are very soft and the broth has nearly evaporated.

2 Stir in the rice, then add the remaining ½ cup broth, the water, black pepper, thyme and basil; bring to a boil. Reduce the heat to low, cover and simmer for 25 to 30 minutes, or until the rice is tender and the liquid has been absorbed.

3 Remove the pan from the heat and transfer the rice to a warmed serving bowl. Sprinkle the rice with the mozzarella.

Preparation time 5 minutes • **Total time** 35 minutes • **Per serving** 105 calories, 0.8 g. fat (7% of calories), 0.3 g. saturated fat, 2 mg. cholesterol, 187 mg. sodium, 0.9 g. dietary fiber, 48 mg. calcium, 1 mg. iron, 5 mg. vitamin C, 0 mg. beta-carotene
Serves 4

To defat canned broth, open the can and place it in the freezer for about 15 minutes. The fat will congeal at the top and then you can easily lift it off.

KITCHEN TIPS
Preshredded cheese saves time in the kitchen, but it tends to be a bit more expensive than a whole piece of cheese. If you shred the mozzarella yourself, spray the grater lightly with no-stick spray and the cheese will slide off easily. Cheese shreds more cleanly when it is well chilled.

FOOD FACT
Converted white rice is soaked and steamed under pressure before it is milled, which helps conserve some of the nutrients. The grains of rice are compressed and hardened in the process, which is why converted rice takes slightly longer to cook than regular white rice.

BAKED SHELLS WITH WHITE CHEDDAR

7 ounces small pasta shells

6 ounces 1% low-fat cottage cheese

1½ cups skim milk

2 tablespoons cornstarch

5 ounces extra-sharp white Cheddar cheese, shredded

½ teaspoon dry mustard

¼ teaspoon freshly ground black pepper

¼ teaspoon hot-pepper sauce or to taste

1 cup frozen leaf spinach, thawed and squeezed dry

¼ cup thinly sliced scallions

1 tablespoon unseasoned dry breadcrumbs

Although it lacks the startling orange color of macaroni and cheese made from a mix, this casserole is loaded with Cheddar flavor. The cheese is melted into a creamy sauce seasoned with mustard and hot sauce to heighten that delicious Cheddary taste. Serve the pasta with juicy slices of perfectly ripe tomato.

1 Preheat the oven to 400°. Spray a 9 x 9-inch baking dish with no-stick spray.

2 Bring a large covered pot of water to a boil over high heat. Add the pasta to the boiling water, return to a boil and cook for 10 to 11 minutes or according to package directions until al dente. Drain the pasta in a colander and rinse briefly under cold running water; drain again.

3 While the pasta is cooking, process the cottage cheese and 1 table-spoon of the milk in a food processor or blender until nearly smooth.

4 Place the remaining milk in a medium, heavy saucepan; whisk in the cornstarch until smooth. Bring to a boil over high heat, stirring constantly; the sauce will be very thick. Transfer the sauce to a large heatproof bowl.

5 Add the puréed cottage-cheese mixture, all but 2 tablespoons of the Cheddar, the mustard, black pepper and hot-pepper sauce to the bowl, and whisk until smooth. Stir in the drained pasta, spinach and scallions.

6 Scrape the pasta mixture into the prepared baking dish; dust the top with the breadcrumbs and the remaining 2 tablespoons Cheddar, and bake for 15 to 20 minutes, or until hot and bubbly.

Preparation time 10 minutes • **Total time** 55 minutes • **Per serving** 430 calories, 13.7 g. fat (29% of calories), 8 g. saturated fat, 41 mg. cholesterol, 507 mg. sodium, 2.6 g. dietary fiber, 472 mg. calcium, 4 mg. iron, 15 mg. vitamin C, 3 mg. beta-carotene • **Serves 4**

PENNE WITH CHICKEN MARENGO

½ cup sun-dried tomatoes (not oil-packed) or 2 tablespoons no-salt-added tomato paste

8 ounces boneless, skinless chicken-breast halves, cut into ½-inch cubes

1 tablespoon all-purpose flour

½ teaspoon dried thyme, crumbled

¼ teaspoon freshly ground black pepper

1 tablespoon olive oil

3 cups sliced fresh mushrooms

½ cup defatted reduced-sodium chicken broth

1 can (16 ounces) crushed tomatoes in purée

½ cup orange juice

1 teaspoon grated orange zest

1 teaspoon brown sugar

⅛ teaspoon salt

8 ounces penne pasta

Legend has it that Napoleon's chef created chicken Marengo for the general after a battlefield victory. Despite its glorious history, it differs very little from a traditional peasant dish of chicken braised with tomatoes and garlic. This version is enlivened with a touch of citrus in the sauce. Served over pasta, it makes a well-rounded meal fit for a victorious soldier—or a busy family.

1 Bring a large covered pot of water to a boil over high heat.

2 Meanwhile, place the dried tomatoes, if using, and 2 cups of water in a small saucepan and bring to a boil over high heat. Remove from the heat and let stand for 5 minutes. Drain the tomatoes in a colander, cool under cold running water and drain again. Using a sharp paring knife or kitchen shears, cut the tomatoes into small pieces; set aside.

3 Toss the chicken cubes with the flour, thyme and black pepper. In a large, heavy skillet, warm the oil over high heat until hot but not smoking. Add the chicken and sauté for 2 to 3 minutes, or until it is golden brown. Add the mushrooms and 2 tablespoons of the broth, and sauté for 2 to 3 minutes, or until the mushrooms are barely tender and have begun to release their juices.

4 Add the cut-up dried tomatoes or the tomato paste, the crushed tomatoes with their purée, the remaining broth, orange juice, orange zest, brown sugar and salt to the skillet, and bring to a boil, scraping the bottom of the pan with a wooden spoon to release the browned bits. Reduce the heat to medium-low and simmer for 8 minutes, or until the sauce is thickened and the flavors are blended.

5 Meanwhile, add the pasta to the boiling water, return to a boil and cook for 12 minutes or according to package directions until al dente; drain in a colander and transfer to a warmed serving bowl.

6 Pour the sauce over the pasta and toss to coat well.

Preparation time 15 minutes • **Total time** 45 minutes • **Per serving** 408 calories, 5.7 g. fat (13% of calories), 0.8 g. saturated fat, 33 mg. cholesterol, 387 mg. sodium, 4.4 g. dietary fiber, 80 mg. calcium, 5 mg. iron, 63 mg. vitamin C, 2 mg. beta-carotene
Serves 4

❧   ❧   ❧

BARLEY-MUSHROOM BAKE

¼ **ounce dried mushrooms (¼ cup)**

¾ **cup boiling water**

1 **cup quartered small fresh mushrooms**

1 **small onion, thinly sliced**

1 **cup defatted reduced-sodium chicken broth**

½ **cup quick-cooking barley**

⅛ **teaspoon freshly ground black pepper or to taste**

Barley comes in many forms, pearled barley being the most familiar. Although the husk and bran are removed in the milling process, pearled barley is still considered a whole grain and is an excellent source of soluble fiber, which helps to lower blood cholesterol. Quick-cooking barley is pearled barley that has been pre-cooked by steaming, and it retains virtually all of its nutritional value.

1 Preheat the oven to 375°.

2 Place the dried mushrooms in a heatproof medium bowl and pour the boiling water over them. Let stand for 4 minutes, or until the mushrooms are soft. Meanwhile, line a small strainer with cheesecloth and suspend it over a cup.

3 Using a slotted spoon, remove the soaked mushrooms from the liquid; chop the mushrooms if the pieces are large. Pour the soaking liquid through the cheesecloth-lined strainer and discard any grit.

4 In a heavy, medium ovenproof saucepan or casserole, combine the fresh mushrooms and onions. Drizzle 1 tablespoon of the broth over them, then sauté over medium-high heat for 3 to 4 minutes, or until the mushrooms are slightly softened; drizzle in 1 tablespoon more broth as the mushrooms and onions cook.

5 Add the remaining broth, the dried mushrooms and strained soaking liquid, the barley and black pepper; bring to a boil over high heat. Cover the pan (if it doesn't have a lid, cover tightly with foil) and bake the casserole for 25 minutes, or until the barley is tender and the liquid has been absorbed.

Preparation time 5 minutes • **Total time** 25 minutes • **Per serving** 90 calories, 0.6 g. fat (6% of calories), 0 g. saturated fat, 0 mg. cholesterol, 162 mg. sodium, 2.6 g. dietary fiber, 12 mg. calcium, 1 mg. iron, 2 mg. vitamin C, 0 mg. beta-carotene
Serves 4

ON THE MENU
This savory side dish is wonderful with roast chicken or turkey breast, taking the place of stuffing (with much less fuss).

The barley is delicious with gravy: Make a low-fat gravy by using defatted chicken broth rather than the fatty drippings from the roasting pan.

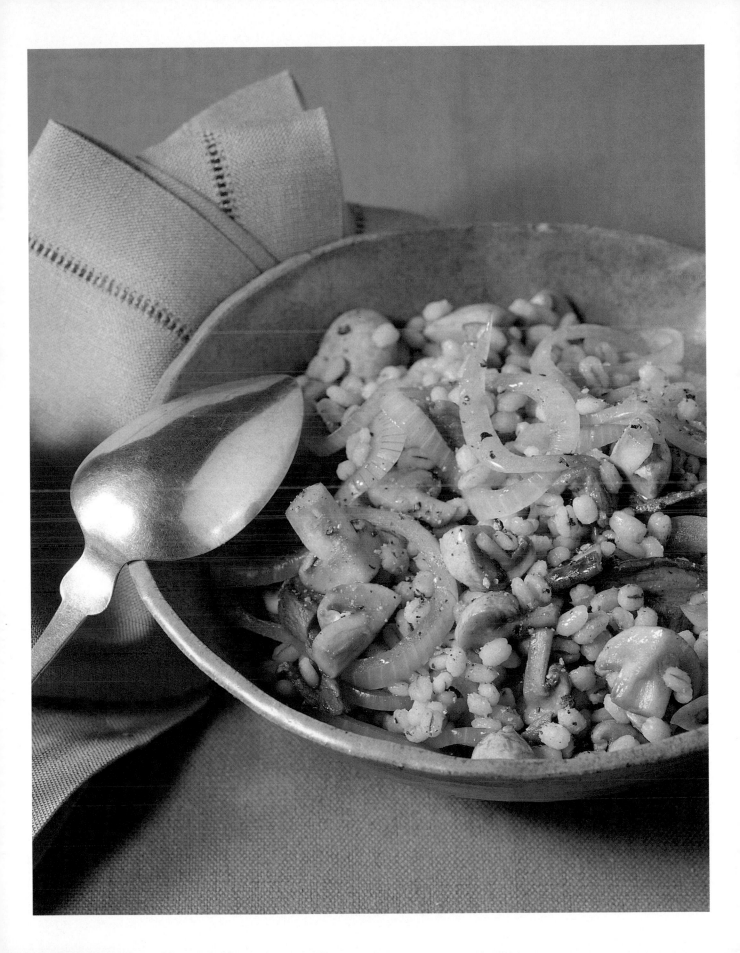

SPAGHETTI WITH GARLIC-LEMON SHRIMP

1 **pound medium shrimp (thawed if frozen), peeled and deveined**

3 **garlic cloves, crushed**

1 **teaspoon grated lemon zest**

¾ **teaspoon dried thyme, crumbled**

¾ **teaspoon dried oregano, crumbled**

½ **teaspoon freshly ground black pepper**

¼ **teaspoon salt**

10 **ounces spaghetti**

2 **teaspoons olive oil**

3 **cups sliced fresh mushrooms**

3 **cans (8 ounces each) no-salt-added tomato sauce**

¼ **cup chopped fresh Italian parsley**

2 **tablespoons grated Parmesan cheese**

After shelling the shrimp, use a paring knife to make a shallow cut in the back of each shrimp, then pull out the black vein.

Shelling shrimp is a simple process; as a bonus, the shells will yield a tasty broth once the job is done (see below). To peel shrimp, slip your thumb under the shell at the larger end of the shrimp and slide it toward the tail to split and remove the shell.

1 Bring a large covered pot of water to a boil over high heat.

2 In a medium bowl, toss the shrimp with the garlic, lemon zest, thyme, oregano, ¼ teaspoon of the black pepper and ⅛ teaspoon of the salt. Cover and let stand at room temperature for 10 minutes.

3 Add the pasta to the boiling water, return the water to a boil and cook for 9 to 11 minutes or according to package directions until al dente. Drain in a colander and transfer to a warmed serving bowl.

4 While the pasta is cooking, in a large, deep no-stick skillet, warm the oil over high heat until very hot. Add the mushrooms and sauté for 2 to 3 minutes, tossing frequently. The pan will be dry at first, but the mushrooms will begin to release their juices as they cook.

5 Add the tomato sauce and the remaining ¼ teaspoon black pepper and ⅛ teaspoon salt to the mushrooms, and bring to a boil. Stir in the shrimp and reduce the heat to medium. Simmer, stirring frequently, for 4 to 5 minutes, or until the shrimp are firm, pink, and opaque throughout.

6 Pour the sauce over the spaghetti; add the parsley and toss to mix, then sprinkle with the Parmesan.

Preparation time 20 minutes • **Total time** 45 minutes • **Per serving** 472 calories, 6.7 g. fat (13% of calories), 1.3 g. saturated fat, 142 mg. cholesterol, 364 mg. sodium, 5.2 g. dietary fiber, 119 mg. calcium, 8 mg. iron, 34 mg. vitamin C, 2 mg. beta-carotene • **Serves 4**

🌿 🌿 🌿

KITCHEN TIPS

The shrimp shells can become the basis of a delicious broth to use when making seafood soups, chowders or sauces. Place the shells in a saucepan with enough cold water to cover; bring to a boil and simmer, covered, for half an hour. Let the shells cool in the broth, then strain them out and freeze the broth in an airtight container for up to six months.

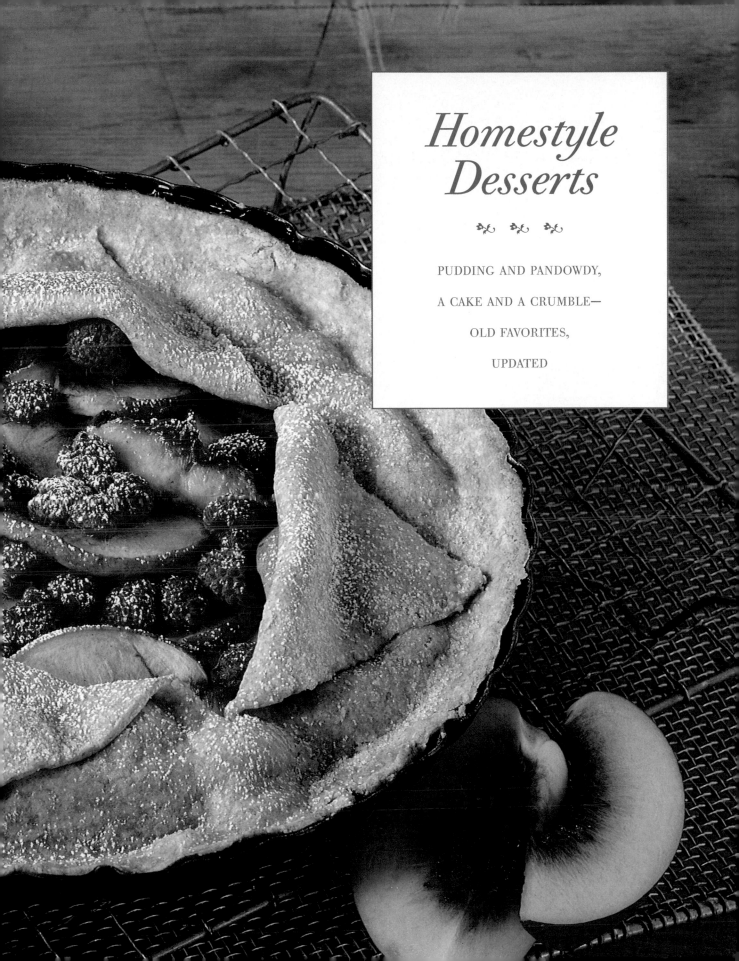

Homestyle Desserts

❧ ❧ ❧

PUDDING AND PANDOWDY,

A CAKE AND A CRUMBLE—

OLD FAVORITES,

UPDATED

Plum Compote with Yogurt Topping

3 tablespoons no-sugar-added raspberry spread

½ teaspoon fresh lemon juice

½ teaspoon vanilla extract

4 ripe medium plums (about 1 pound), cut into ½-inch wedges

Half of a 3-inch cinnamon stick or a pinch of ground cinnamon

1 cup nonfat vanilla frozen yogurt

Compotes can be made with either fresh or dried fruits, or a combination of the two. Dried fruits require slow cooking to soften; on the other hand, you have to be careful not to over-cook fresh fruits—such as the plums used in this recipe—or they may disintegrate. The cooking time will depend on the variety of plums you choose and on their ripeness.

1 In a heavy, medium saucepan, combine the raspberry spread, lemon juice and vanilla, and stir until syrupy. Add the plums and cinnamon stick or ground cinnamon, and toss gently with a rubber spatula until the fruit is coated with the syrup. Place the pan over medium heat and bring to a simmer, stirring frequently but gently. Reduce the heat to medium-low, cover and simmer for 8 to 12 minutes, or until the plums are very tender. Remove the cinnamon stick, if using.

2 Spoon the cooked plums into 4 dessert dishes and place them in the refrigerator to chill for 20 minutes (to save time, you can chill the plums in the freezer for about 10 minutes).

3 Top each dish of plums with some of the frozen yogurt.

In late summer and early fall, you'll find many varieties of plums to choose from at local farm markets and supermarkets.

Preparation time 5 minutes • **Total time** 15 minutes • **Per serving** 142 calories, 0.7 g. fat (4% of calories), 0 g. saturated fat, 0 mg. cholesterol, 23 mg. sodium, 2.2 g. dietary fiber, 55 mg. calcium, 0 mg. iron, 10 mg. vitamin C, 0.2 mg. beta-carotene • **Serves 4**

FOOD FACT

Most of the commercially grown plums in the United States come from California. Some of the most popular varieties shipped from that state are the amber-fleshed El Dorado, super-sweet Laroda, mahogany-skinned Queen Anne and gold-fleshed Casselman, as well as Friars, Simkas, Black Beauts and big, meaty Elephant Heart plums, which are particularly good for cooking. These California fruits are all Japanese varieties, which are generally plump, round and juicy, with skins ranging from yellow to crimson to black. European plums, grown in other parts of the country, are more egg-shaped and usually have purple-blue skins and drier, denser flesh than their Japanese counterparts. The large, sweet Jefferson, Washington and President plums, small Italian prune plums and the poetically named Tragedy are among the better-known European varieties. Many of these European plums are freestone.

Preceding pages: Nectarine and Raspberry Pandowdy (recipe on page 119)

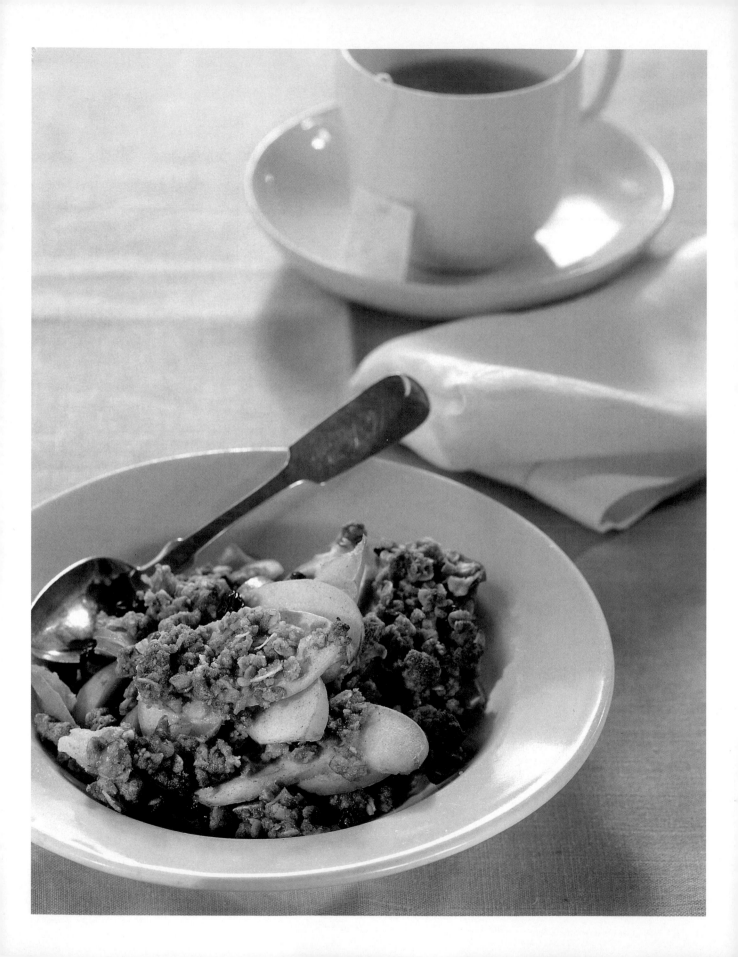

APPLE-OATMEAL CRUMBLE

½ **cup old-fashioned rolled oats**

2 **tablespoons all-purpose flour**

2 **tablespoons whole-wheat flour**

2 **tablespoons packed dark brown sugar**

1 **teaspoon ground cinnamon**

 Pinch of salt

1 **tablespoon plus 2 teaspoons cold unsalted butter or margarine, cut into small pieces**

3 **large Granny Smith apples, cored and quartered**

¼ **cup frozen apple juice concentrate, thawed**

3 **tablespoons dried currants**

1 **tablespoon honey**

1 **teaspoon fresh lemon juice**

A pastry blender with wire "tines" is the perfect tool for cutting butter or margarine into dry ingredients.

irm, well-flavored apples that hold their shape when heated—rather than turning to applesauce—are best for baking. The versatile Granny Smith and the Golden Delicious (both popular for eating raw, as well) are excellent in baked desserts. You can use just about any type of apple in this crumble, but be prepared to adjust the seasonings according to the flavor of the apples. Very tart varieties, such as Rhode Island Greenings, may call for a bit more sugar, while bland McIntoshes could probably use a touch more lemon juice and spice—or even a few drops of vanilla extract.

1 Preheat the oven to 450°.

2 In a medium bowl, stir together the oats, all-purpose flour, whole-wheat flour, brown sugar, ½ teaspoon of the cinnamon and the salt. Using your fingers or a pastry blender, lightly mix in the butter or margarine until coarse crumbs form; set aside.

3 In a food processor fitted with the slicing blade, or by hand, thinly slice the apples.

4 Place the apples in another medium bowl; add the remaining ½ teaspoon cinnamon, the apple juice concentrate, currants, honey and lemon juice, and toss until well mixed. Transfer the apple mixture to a 9-inch deep-dish pie plate and top with the crumb mixture.

5 Bake for 10 minutes, or until the topping begins to brown in patches. Reduce the oven temperature to 400°, cover the crumble loosely with foil, and bake for 15 to 20 minutes longer, or until the apples are tender and the filling is bubbly. Place the pan on a wire rack to cool slightly and serve the crumble warm.

Preparation time 15 minutes • **Total time** 45 minutes • **Per serving** 185 calories, 4.1 g. fat (20% of calories), 2.1 g. saturated fat, 9 mg. cholesterol, 28 mg. sodium, 3.2 g. dietary fiber, 27 mg. calcium, 1 mg. iron, 16 mg. vitamin C, 0 mg. beta-carotene
Serves 6

APPLESAUCE GINGERBREAD

2 cups all-purpose flour

1½ teaspoons ground cinnamon

1¼ teaspoons baking powder

1 teaspoon ground nutmeg

¾ teaspoon ground ginger

¼ teaspoon baking soda

⅛ teaspoon ground cloves

⅛ teaspoon salt

Pinch of ground cardamom (optional)

¼ cup packed dark brown sugar

¼ cup dark molasses

1 large egg

1 tablespoon vegetable oil

1 cup unsweetened applesauce

1 teaspoon vanilla extract

½ cup chopped Golden Delicious apples

1 tablespoon frozen apple juice concentrate, thawed

No fewer than six distinct spices give this glossy-topped gingerbread a pleasing pungency you won't find in any packaged mix. The applesauce in the batter replaces much of the shortening in a standard gingerbread recipe—a trick that can be used in many simple cakes and quick breads. Chopped apples are also added to the batter, and when the cake comes out of the oven, the top is glazed with apple juice concentrate for a triple "hit" of apple flavor.

1 Preheat the oven to 375°. Spray an 8-inch round cake pan with no-stick spray.

2 In a large bowl, stir together the flour, cinnamon, baking powder, nutmeg, ginger, baking soda, cloves, salt and cardamom, if using; set aside.

3 In a medium bowl, whisk together the brown sugar, molasses, egg and oil until smooth. Stir in the applesauce and vanilla.

4 Scrape the applesauce mixture into the flour mixture and stir until well blended. Fold in the apples.

5 Pour the batter into the prepared pan and smooth the top. Bake for 30 to 35 minutes, or until the top of the cake is springy to the touch and a toothpick inserted just off center comes out clean. Transfer the pan to a wire rack and cool for 10 minutes.

6 Run a knife around the edge of the cake to loosen it, then turn the cake out onto a rack; immediately invert it onto a serving plate so it is right-side up. Brush the top of the cake with the apple juice concentrate.

7 To serve, cut the cake into wedges.

Preparation time 25 minutes • **Total time** 55 minutes • **Per serving** 215 calories, 2.9 g. fat (12% of calories), 0.5 g. saturated fat, 27 mg. cholesterol, 168 mg. sodium, 1.4 g. dietary fiber, 152 mg. calcium, 4 mg. iron, 3 mg. vitamin C, 0 mg. beta-carotene
Serves 8

Ambrosia Parfaits

2 tablespoons sweetened
shredded coconut

2 medium navel oranges

½ cup halved seedless red grapes

½ cup drained crushed juice-pack
pineapple, 1 tablespoon
juice reserved

1 pint nonfat vanilla frozen
yogurt, slightly softened

Mint sprigs for garnish
(optional)

Layers of sliced oranges, grated coconut and confectioners' sugar are combined to make the dessert that Southerners call "ambrosia." Traditionalists might see this recipe as gilding the lily, but layering oranges, pineapple, grapes and coconut with frozen yogurt does create a truly irresistible treat.

1 Place the coconut in a small no-stick skillet. Toast over medium heat, tossing frequently, for 2 to 3 minutes, or until lightly browned. Transfer the coconut to a small plate to cool.

2 Using a sharp paring knife, remove the peel and white pith from the oranges. Cut the oranges crosswise into ½-inch-thick slices, then chop coarsely. Transfer the chopped oranges to a bowl, add the grapes and the pineapple with its reserved juice, and mix.

3 Divide one-third of the fruit mixture among four 10- to 12-ounce parfait glasses or dessert dishes. Using half of the yogurt, spoon a layer of yogurt over the fruit. Alternate layers of the remaining fruit mixture and yogurt in the glasses, ending with the fruit mixture. Sprinkle the parfaits with the toasted coconut and garnish with mint sprigs, if desired.

Preparation time 10 minutes • **Total time** 15 minutes • **Per serving** 169 calories, 0.9 g. fat (5% of calories), 0.7 g. saturated fat, 0 mg. cholesterol, 52 mg. sodium, 2.1 g. dietary fiber, 134 mg. calcium, 0 mg. iron, 44 mg. vitamin C, 0.1 mg. beta-carotene • **Serves 4**

❧ ❧ ❧

Cut off the tops and bottoms of the oranges, then pare downward in wide strips, removing all of the white pith.

Cut each pared orange crosswise into ½-inch-thick slices, then coarsely chop the sliced oranges.

Nectarine and Raspberry Pandowdy

⅓ cup whole-wheat flour

¼ cup all-purpose flour

⅛ teaspoon salt

2 tablespoons cold unsalted butter or margarine, cut into small pieces

2 tablespoons ice water

¼ cup frozen apple juice concentrate, thawed

2 tablespoons cornstarch

1 tablespoon plus 1 teaspoon granulated sugar

¼ teaspoon ground cinnamon

¼ teaspoon ground mace or nutmeg

2 pounds ripe nectarines, cut into ¼-inch-thick slices

1 cup fresh or frozen unsweetened raspberries

1 teaspoon skim milk

1 teaspoon confectioners' sugar for garnish (optional)

To save time peeling the fruit, choose large nectarines. When fresh nectarines are out of season, make this tart-sweet dessert with unsweetened frozen peach slices.

1 Preheat the oven to 425°.

2 In a medium bowl, stir together the whole-wheat flour, all-purpose flour and salt. Mix in the butter or margarine with your fingers or two knives. Stir in enough of the ice water to form a soft dough.

3 Shape the dough into a flat disk and place it between 2 sheets of wax paper. Roll the dough out into a 9-inch circle. Chill the dough while you prepare the filling.

4 In a large bowl, mix the apple juice concentrate, cornstarch, 1 tablespoon of the granulated sugar, the cinnamon and mace or nutmeg. Add the nectarines and toss to mix well. Spoon the filling into a 9½-inch deep-dish pie plate and scatter the raspberries on top.

5 Remove the dough from the refrigerator and peel off the top sheet of wax paper. Invert the dough over the fruit and peel off the second sheet of paper. Cut a large X in the center of the dough and turn back the points so they almost touch the edges of the crust. Brush the crust with the milk and sprinkle with the remaining 1 teaspoon granulated sugar. Place the pie plate on a baking sheet.

6 Bake the pandowdy for 12 to 15 minutes, or until the crust is lightly browned; reduce the oven temperature to 375° and bake for 15 to 20 minutes longer, turning the dish if the crust browns unevenly. The crust should be crisp and browned and the fruit tender and bubbly.

7 Cool the pandowdy on a wire rack, then sprinkle it with confectioners' sugar, if desired. To serve, cut the crust into 8 wedges; spoon the filling onto dessert plates and top with wedges of crust.

Preparation time 25 minutes • **Total time** 55 minutes plus cooling time
Per serving 146 calories, 3.6 g. fat (22% of calories), 1.8 g. saturated fat, 8 mg. cholesterol, 38 mg. sodium, 3.1 g. dietary fiber, 15 mg. calcium, 1 mg. iron, 17 mg. vitamin C, 0.5 mg. beta-carotene • **Serves 8**

BAKED CHOCOLATE PUDDING

1 cup skim milk

1 cup 1% low-fat milk

⅓ cup unsweetened Dutch-process cocoa powder, plus ½ teaspoon cocoa powder for garnish

¼ cup granulated sugar

2 tablespoons cornstarch

Pinch of salt

1 large egg

1 large egg white

2 teaspoons vanilla extract

1½ ounces semisweet chocolate, cut up

Chocolate pudding is not just for kids: This velvety baked pudding has a sophisticated semisweet flavor that grownups will love. Since the recipe calls for only 1½ ounces of chocolate, you could treat yourself to a fine European brand; however, a domestic semisweet baking chocolate—even chocolate chips—will make an excellent pudding, too. Baking the ramekins of pudding in a pan of hot water protects them from the direct heat of the oven, ensuring that they cook slowly and evenly with little chance of burning.

1 Preheat the oven to 350°.

2 Pour the skim milk and low-fat milk into a small, heavy saucepan and warm over medium heat until small bubbles form around the edges; do not boil the milk.

3 Sift the ⅓ cup cocoa into a medium heatproof bowl. Stir in the sugar, cornstarch and salt. Add the whole egg, egg white and vanilla, and whisk until smooth.

4 Pour the hot milk into a large glass measuring cup or heatproof pitcher. Gradually whisk the hot milk into the cocoa mixture. Add the chocolate and whisk until melted.

5 Pour the mixture into the measuring cup and divide it among four 7- to 8-ounce ramekins or custard cups.

6 Set the ramekins in a 9 x 13-inch baking pan and add hot water to reach ½ inch up the sides of the ramekins. Bake for 30 to 35 minutes, or until the puddings are set; they should not jiggle when the baking pan is shaken gently. Remove the puddings from the water bath and transfer to a wire rack to cool until barely warm.

7 Serve the puddings warm, or refrigerate for 2 to 3 hours and serve chilled. Dust the puddings with the remaining ½ teaspoon cocoa.

Preparation time 15 minutes • **Total time** 55 minutes • **Per serving** 210 calories, 6.5 g. fat (28% of calories), 3.4 g. saturated fat, 57 mg. cholesterol, 177 mg. sodium, 0 g. dietary fiber, 170 mg. calcium, 1 mg. iron, 1 mg. vitamin C, 0 mg. beta-carotene
Serves 4

∂ᶜ ∂ᶜ ∂ᶜ

HONEY-BAKED PEARS

2 bags apple-cinnamon tea
(herbal tea)

1¼ cups boiling water

4 small firm-ripe pears (about
1 pound, 10 ounces)

3 tablespoons golden or dark
raisins

2 tablespoons honey

1½ teaspoons fresh lemon juice

1½ teaspoons vanilla extract

Caffeine-free teas—herbal or fruit-flavored—are a perfect medium for poaching fruit, especially if you choose complementary combinations such as apple-cinnamon tea with apples or pears, or almond tea with plums, peaches or cherries. In this recipe, honey, lemon and vanilla enhance the mellow taste of the pears.

1 Preheat the oven to 425°.

2 Place the tea bags in a small heatproof bowl and add the boiling water. Cover and steep for 5 minutes.

3 Meanwhile, peel and core the pears; cut them into ¼-inch-thick wedges. Arrange the pears in an 11 x 7-inch baking dish and sprinkle the raisins over them.

4 Remove the tea bags and stir the honey, lemon juice and vanilla into the tea. Pour the tea mixture over the pears and cover the dish with foil. Bake for 20 to 25 minutes, or until the pears are tender.

5 Remove the baking dish, uncover it and let the pears cool until just warm. Serve the pears with the raisins and pan juices.

After halving the pears, scoop out the cores with a teaspoon or melon baller.

Preparation time 15 minutes • **Total time** 40 minutes • **Per serving** 160 calories, 0.7 g. fat (4% of calories), 0 g. saturated fat, 0 mg. cholesterol, 2 mg. sodium, 4.8 g. dietary fiber, 23 mg. calcium, 0 mg. iron, 8 mg. vitamin C, 0 mg. beta-carotene • **Serves 4**

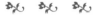

FOR A CHANGE
Try flavoring the pears with dark rum rather than vanilla extract. Substitute chopped dried figs for the raisins.

ON THE MENU
Baked pears are a deliciously light alternative to pie at holiday dinners. Dress up the dish with a dollop of frozen yogurt and serve the pears with crisp wafer cookies.

MARKET AND PANTRY
Pears are usually picked slightly under-ripe, so they often need some time to ripen after you buy them. Choose unblemished pears, and leave them at room temperature for a few days. When ripe, the pears will be fragrant and will give to gentle pressure at the stem end. Some varieties, such as Bartletts and Clapps, develop a rosy "blush" as they ripen.

APRICOT BREAD PUDDING

⅓ **cup snipped dried apricot halves**

½ **cup boiling water**

2 **cups skim milk**

¼ **cup no-sugar-added apricot preserves**

2 **large eggs**

2 **large egg whites**

2 **tablespoons granulated sugar**

1 **tablespoon cornstarch**

1 **tablespoon frozen orange juice concentrate**

1½ **teaspoons vanilla extract**

3 **cups crusty bread cubes (½-inch cubes), preferably cracked-wheat or whole-wheat French peasant bread**

Bread pudding was presumably created as a way to use up left-over bread, but the dessert belies its humble beginnings. In a glorified version of French toast, the bread is combined with milk and eggs, sugar and fruit, and then baked into a cakelike confection. Coarse-textured whole-grain peasant bread makes a particularly satisfying pudding; you can also use a regular French loaf.

1 Preheat the oven to 375°. Spray a 9 x 9-inch baking dish with no-stick spray. Place the apricots in a small heatproof bowl, pour the boiling water over them and set aside to plump for 5 to 10 minutes.

2 Meanwhile, in a blender or food processor, combine the milk, apricot preserves, eggs, egg whites, sugar, cornstarch, orange juice concentrate and vanilla, and process until well combined.

3 Drain the plumped apricots and place them, along with the bread cubes, in the prepared baking dish. Pour in the milk mixture and mix well with a rubber spatula.

4 Bake for 30 to 35 minutes, or until the pudding is set and the top is puffed and lightly browned. Place the pan on a wire rack to cool slightly; serve the pudding warm. Refrigerate any leftovers.

Preparation time 15 minutes • **Total time** 50 minutes • **Per serving** 135 calories, 2 g. fat (13% of calories), 0.6 g. saturated fat, 54 mg. cholesterol, 133 mg. sodium, 1.1 g. dietary fiber, 91 mg. calcium, 1 mg. iron, 4 mg. vitamin C, 0.2 mg. beta-carotene • **Serves 8**

Kitchen shears make quick work of cutting up dried apricots. Spray the blades lightly with no-stick spray to make the job even easier.

NUTRITION NOTE

Dried apricots are among the most concentrated sources of beta-carotene; these tangy-sweet fruits also provide good amounts of potassium, iron and dietary fiber. Apricots, like other dried fruits, may be treated with sulfur dioxide to preserve their color. If you're allergic to sulfites, look for unsulfured apricots at a health-food store or gourmet shop.

FOR A CHANGE

Make the bread pudding with other dried fruits, such as dark or golden raisins, snipped prunes or figs, or dried cherries. If using cherries or figs, substitute pure almond extract for the vanilla.

HEAD START

Cut up the bread in advance and let the bread cubes dry for a few hours.

INDEX

❧ ❧ ❧